Purr-fect Recipes

for a Healthy Cat

101 Natural Cat Food & Treat Recipes
to Make Your Cat Happy

By

Lisa Shiroff

Purr-fect Recipes for a Healthy Cat: 101 Natural Cat Food & Treat Recipes to Make Your Cat Happy

Library of Congress Cataloging-in-Publication Data

Shiroff, Lisa, 1968-
Purr-fect recipes for a healthy cat : 101 natural cat food & treat recipes to make your cat happy / by Lisa Shiroff.
    p. cm.
Includes bibliographical references and index.
ISBN-13: 978-1-60138-398-3 (alk. paper)
ISBN-10: 1-60138-398-3 (alk. paper)
 1. Cats--Nutrition. 2. Cats--Food--Recipes. I. Title.
SF447.6.S55 2010
636.8'085--dc22

                              2010039585

PEER REVIEWER: Marilee Griffin • PROJECT MANAGER: Sylvia Maye • INTERIOR DESIGN: Dolores McElroy
PROOFREADER: C&P Marse • bluemoon6749@bellsouth.net
FRONT COVER DESIGN: Meg Buchner • megadesn@mchsi.com
BACK COVER DESIGN: Jackie Miller • millerjackiej@gmail.com

Printed on Recycled Paper

Printed in the United States

We recently lost our beloved pet "Bear," who was not only our best and dearest friend but also the "Vice President of Sunshine" here at Atlantic Publishing. He did not receive a salary but worked tirelessly 24 hours a day to please his parents. Bear was a rescue dog that turned around and showered myself, my wife, Sherri, his grandparents Jean, Bob, and Nancy, and every person and animal he met (maybe not rabbits) with friendship and love. He made a lot of people smile every day.

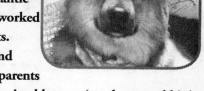

We wanted you to know that a portion of the profits of this book will be donated to The Humane Society of the United States.   *–Douglas & Sherri Brown*

The human-animal bond is as old as human history. We cherish our animal companions for their unconditional affection and acceptance. We feel a thrill when we glimpse wild creatures in their natural habitat or in our own backyard.

Unfortunately, the human-animal bond has at times been weakened. Humans have exploited some animal species to the point of extinction.

The Humane Society of the United States makes a difference in the lives of animals here at home and worldwide. The HSUS is dedicated to creating a world where our relationship with animals is guided by compassion. We seek a truly humane society in which animals are respected for their intrinsic value, and where the human-animal bond is strong.

Want to help animals? We have plenty of suggestions. Adopt a pet from a local shelter, join The Humane Society and be a part of our work to help companion animals and wildlife. You will be funding our educational, legislative, investigative and outreach projects in the U.S. and across the globe.

Or perhaps you'd like to make a memorial donation in honor of a pet, friend or relative? You can through our Kindred Spirits program. And if you'd like to contribute in a more structured way, our Planned Giving Office has suggestions about estate planning, annuities, and even gifts of stock that avoid capital gains taxes.

Maybe you have land that you would like to preserve as a lasting habitat for wildlife. Our Wildlife Land Trust can help you. Perhaps the land you want to share is a backyard—that's enough. Our Urban Wildlife Sanctuary Program will show you how to create a habitat for your wild neighbors.

So you see, it's easy to help animals. And The HSUS is here to help.

THE HUMANE SOCIETY OF THE UNITED STATES.

2100 L Street NW • Washington, DC 20037 • 202-452-1100
www.hsus.org

DEDICATION

This book is dedicated to my husband for his unconditional love and tolerance of my impulsiveness.

TABLE OF CONTENTS

INTRODUCTION

Hello, cat owner! Luna was a beautiful seal-point Siamese cat. Originally, my mother named her after the Roman goddess of the moon. But after she developed some rather peculiar eating habits, my father dropped the divine connection and started telling people that her name was shortened from Lunatic-People-Own-Her. Why? Because she refused to eat cat food and my mother catered to her very discriminating tastes. Luna would turn up her nose at anything that came from a commercially sealed container. Regardless of how promising the aroma coming from the can was, oblivious to the expense of the kibble rattling into her crystal dish, she would allow herself only the smallest of nibbles before sauntering off with nary a glance at the humans standing by muttering: "Now what are we going to feed her?"

Eventually my family noticed how affectionate Luna became when we would eat our own meals around the dinner table. She would purr and rub herself against our legs and weave about the chairs. She would make eye contact with us every time her head peaked out from beneath the tabletop. Finally, we understood her behavior. We realized what she was trying to tell us: She wanted some of our food. Mom tested the waters by feeding her some baked chicken taken from the casserole dish on the stove, and forever after, Luna ate what we humans in the house ate.

Luna is not the only cat to prefer traditional, "human" food to the modern commercial preparations that are so readily available today. Cats and humans have been sharing meat and vegetables for centuries. It all began about 4,000 years ago when someone, probably in a kitchen, stepped aside and let a cat walk into a house. It took a few hundred years, but eventually a deal was made. A permanent relationship was created, and ever since, humans have kept and fed domesticated cats in their homes. It is a matter of perspective, of course. If you ask a cat, she will tell you it was felines who let humans cohabit with them.

Regardless of which side you are on, it is generally agreed that cats and humans started living comfortably together in ancient Egypt where — as the cat will point out — felines were also worshipped as gods. Since that time, the domestic cat found its way into the hearts and homes of Europeans. Eventually, cats were brought to North America with the New England colonists. And now, according to the American Pet Products Manufacturers Association in a 2009 – 2010 National Pet Owners Survey, there are more than 93 million pet cats in the United States alone. There are more cats than any other pet animal in the country. There are more pet cats in the United States than there are people in most European countries. Of course, felines do not need a survey to tell them they are the preferred pet because they have always known where their rightful place should be — at the top of the popularity totem pole. And many have even attempted to tell canines.

Famous cats in history

For some reason cats are generally left out of the academic history books. To make amends for that error, the following list contains some of the most famous cats in recorded history.

- Boche was the cat Anne Frank's family found in the attic where they lived.

- Blackie became the world's richest cat when he inherited 15 million pounds from his British owner, Ben Rea.

- Dusty was a tabby from Texas who set the record in 1952 for having more kittens than any other cat. The famous queen managed to bring more than 420 kittens into the world, having her last litter when she was 18.

- Faith is the only non-military animal to receive the PDSA Silver Medal for her bravery during wartime when she stayed in St. Faith and St. Augustine's church to take care of her kitten while the church was repeatedly being bombed.

- Fred became famous when he went "undercover" to help the New York Police Department arrest a suspect accused of posing as a veterinarian.

- Midnight was a cat that belonged to Bernice and Roy Rogers. He became a hero by saving their daughter's life.

- Nedgem is reportedly the first pet cat to ever have a name. He lived in ancient Egypt during the time of Pharaoh Thutmose III (1479 BC to 1425 BC).

- Siam was the first Siamese cat to land on the shores of the United States. He was a gift for President Rutherford B. Hayes from the American consul in Bangkok.

- Tabby was the first pet cat to live in the White House. He belonged to Abraham Lincoln's son, Tad.

- Tiger, another presidential cat, belonged to Theodore Roosevelt, who would walk around the White House with Tiger draped around his neck.

- Towser was designated the world's best mouser. She "worked" for the Glenturret Distillery in Scotland where she caught 28,899 mice along with an unknown number of rats, rabbits, and other unlucky rodents.

The relationship between humans and cats probably resulted when humans realized how helpful a cat could be around the house, particularly when it comes to keeping rodents away. Perhaps the cats were amused by the way humans would shriek at the tiny, furry mice and rats while they, the pristine feline species, showed off their daring prowess and stalking abilities. But soon enough, humans discovered other endearing feline qualities, and cats became a preferred animal companion. We adore them as they purr on our laps. We enjoy the way they play with balls of yarn at our feet. And we look on in envy as they stretch out in the sunbeams slanting across our living rooms. Now we no longer see cats as necessary — and cute — forms of pest control. We see them as valuable members of our families. As such, we want to give them the best life they can, which includes feeding them well. There is no more important way we can impact our cat's quality of life and influence its health than by choosing its diet.

Cats do have distinct food and nutritional requirements. For decades, humans have tried to figure out just how to cater those needs. To make it easier for cat owners to meet those requirements, pet food companies began making commercial cat foods on a massive scale in the 1930s. Since then, grocery shelves and pet supply stores have offered a variety of cat food and treats to fit every American budget and lifestyle. And while it certainly is easy to pop open a can of prepared, processed food or rip open a bag of kibble, the convenience might not be a good trade-off for the benefits more natural foods provide. Many of those commercial foods have ingredients and fillers that may not be in the best interest of your cat's health. Several contain chemical preservatives, rendered animal fat (for example, restaurant grease), artificial food coloring, sugar, and other sweeteners that humans refuse to eat in their own foods. Other pet food products contain meat and by-products that are unfit for human consumption, such as chicken feet or horse intestines. Compounding those issues is the possibility of yet another pet food recall after too many cats were sickened by improperly, even dangerously, prepared commercial cat food. Is that the kind of food you really want to feed the companion who likes to lie on your chest while you read? Perhaps even now, while you are reading this book?

During the late 1970s and early 1980s, humans started to re-examine the concept of what is required to live a healthy life. The "fitness craze" began encouraging people to exercise and adopt diet and lifestyle changes that would help them achieve optimum levels of good health. As a result, a variety of diet recommendations and diverse eating regimens were developed to fit every palate, fitness level, and health issue any American had. And while we are now able to hone in on individual dietary needs and custom tailor our meals to fulfill those needs, a common ideal is becoming prevalent among most of us: A healthy diet consists of a variety of fresh, whole foods made of natural ingredients. Those foods provide more nutrition, purer forms of energy, and are less toxic to our bodies and the earth than are the prepackaged, highly refined products favored by previous generations. Perhaps it only makes sense that as we pet parents become more health conscious and strive to eat a diet based on whole, natural foods, we feel it is right and fair, perhaps even a moral obligation, to try and do the same for our pets.

If you find you are attracted to the idea of creating a natural food diet for your cat, then *Purr-fect Recipes for a Healthy Cat: 101 Natural Cat Food & Treat Recipes to Make Your Cat Happy* will get you started. You will learn about your cat's nutritional needs and her specific requirements for the basic meal components of protein, fat, and carbohydrates. You will understand how the amount of moisture in your feline's food plays a key role in her health, unlike with other animals. You will also discover the unique nutritional needs of your cat, such as for the essential amino acid taurine, which are integral to his or her development and good health. This book will discuss how a cat's body easily digests some foods but has difficulty processing others, and the health issues that may arise as a result. Other medical conditions that target cats in particular will also be explored along with nutritional tips and ideas for easing the discomfort that comes along with those conditions.

At the core of the book is the concept that a natural food diet can be healthier and more beneficial for your cat than feeding him or her a diet of commercial, processed foods. A natural food diet can also be just as convenient as packaged cat food, as the meals you make for your favorite tabby are often created from the same foods you purchase for yourself, your mate, and the human members of your litter. To that end, this book will teach you how to incorporate preparing meals and cooking for your cat into your life, so the change is easier on you. It will also discuss methods of changing your cat's diet in a way that will not upset him or her, but it will encourage enjoyment of the new sumptuous, royal feasts so rightly deserved.

Of course, you will also find 101 delectable recipes that will help you make the switch from commercial foods to all-natural ones. We have supplied you with a variety of recipes for treats, meal components, full meals, and even a few supplements. You will also find a shopping list, a list of useful kitchen items (many of which you probably already have in your household), and an inventory of foods you must avoid because they are toxic to your cat.

We understand how much your beloved feline family member means to you. We did our best to provide you with the most up-to-date information on cat nutrition and cat health. But, we do not personally know your cat. It is important that you remember, when making any changes to your cat's diet, you must discuss the idea with your veterinarian. Though each cat knows she is the greatest cat in the world, each one is also different, and many have particular needs or conditions that can be affected by a change in her diet. It is imperative you keep your cat's veterinarian informed of any changes you intend to make.

Knowing you can take control of your cat's diet to enhance the quality of her life and — quite possibly — improve the quality of her health is empowering. Now, hopefully your appetite for change is whetted, so let us start whetting your cat's appetite for better food. Find your apron, and roll up your sleeves, it is time to start cranking out some "purr-fect recipes" for your cat.

CHAPTER 1

The Healthy Cat

Through the ages cats have developed a reputation for being indestructible. It is said they have nine lives. People believe cats always land on their feet, regardless of how far they fall; they laud the alley cat for the ability to survive fights with the toughest of dogs. But the truth of the matter is a cat is only as healthy and strong as his or her living conditions and his or her diet, in particular, will allow.

A well-fed cat is easily distinguishable. The cat's weight, the thickness and sheen of the coat, and the sturdiness of his or her build are all impacted by the amount and quality of the food eaten. Energy levels and motor coordination require a cat-particular ratio of protein-to-fats-to-carbohydrates. The nutrient density of food can help prevent disease, and likewise, if the food's nutrition is inadequate, it will encourage disease. If you are going to help your cat attain the highest levels of health and wellness possible, you must be aware of the foods you choose to feed him or her. You must understand how they affect your cat, and choose them accordingly.

What is in a name?

Readers may notice that often a male cat is made reference to by the term "tom" but there does not seem to be a female nickname used within this text, which begs the question: If a male cat is called a tom, then what is a female cat called?

It may seem unfortunately banal, but a female cat is simply called a she-cat. Those girls make up for it though when they are pregnant or nursing kittens. During that stage of a she-cat's life, she is called a "queen."

To clarify other cat terms used here: Whether it is a male or a female, a tabby is a cat with stripes or brindled colors. It is not a breed. The word is derived from the Arabic word "attabiya," which comes from "Attabiy," an ancient Baghdad neighborhood once famous for making striped cloth. Meanwhile, the rather cumbersome and less regal-sounding word, ailurophile describes humans who are cat lovers.

And while on the subject of cat name calling . . .

A group of kittens is called a "kindle."

A group of grown cats is called a "clowder."

"Pride" is usually reserved to refer to a group of large, wild cats.

"Colony" is saved for a group of feral cats.

And a group of cat-loving humans is called "a group of cat-loving humans."

What a Healthy Cat Looks Like

You can easily tell a healthy cat by his or her appearance. With proper diet and exercise, the cat will have a strong, solid body. The hair will be sleek and shiny on a shorthaired cat and thick and soft if long-haired. The eyes and ears will be clear of discharge, and teeth will be white and sharp. There will be no evidence of parasites or pest infestations, or any flaking or scaling of his or her skin. And a healthy cat is spritely and nimble in movement.

Weight

There are two types of body classification for cats. One is the cobby type. A cat with a cobby-style body will have relatively short legs and tail, a broad head, shoulders and hindquarters, deep chest, and round head. The Persian and the British Shorthair are breeds that exemplify the cobby body type, as do most alley cats and domestic breeds of uncertain heritage. The other body type is the foreign body, also called the Oriental. Siamese cats are indicative of this breed. They are slender with a narrow head and long legs and tail. The foreign body type will also have taller ears and more slanting eyes than the cobby. Regardless of your cat's body type, the signs of obesity and underweight are the same.

If your cat is overweight, his or her sides will alternately bulge out when walking. When you stand above him or her and look down, you will notice an obvious distention of the sides of the stomach. An overweight cat will also have "love handles" on its back near the rump and pockets of fat around his or her face. And he or she will be caught lounging in a sunbeam more often than exploring the top of the bookshelves.

A danger for obese cats that many pet owners do not realize is that if a cat becomes so overweight that the girth is wider than the expanse of the whiskers, it will be at risk for losing its sense of perception. One of the primary reasons your cat has whiskers is to figure out whether he or she can fit into a space. If you have ever observed a cat slowly stick his or her head into an area before going all the way in, you would have seen him or her testing the limits of the space to determine if it can fit. Because cat whiskers only grow to a preset length, they will not expand along with the tummy. Hence, overweight cats are at risk of getting stuck between stairway railings, partially under furniture, or in worse predicaments because their heads fit, and they do not realize their bodies do not.

On the other hand, if cats are underweight, instead of a bulging around the midsection, their sides will look concave, indented behind the ribs. The ribs and spine will be noticeable, and hair will feel thin and coarse. In fact, the hair will be more likely to look as if it is standing on end, than it will to appear sleek and lying flat. In addition to affecting their girth, being underweight causes kittens to suffer from stunted growth and premature development. One thing an underweight cat has in common with an overweight cat is that propensity to sit or lie still. Underweight cats just do not have the energy of a cat of prime weight.

A cat at a healthy weight will have only a thin layer of fat along his or her sides and down the back. As you run your hand along the body, you will barely notice the spine and ribs. When you look down on a healthy cat from directly above him or her, the waistline will have only a slight narrowing where the ribs end. A typical, full-grown adult domestic cat weighs between 8 and 10 pounds, but magically appears weightless as he or she soars up above the kitchen cabinets to survey the domain.

Record-breaking cats

Himmy, a cat in Queensland, Australia, is generally considered the heaviest domestic cat on record. Weighing in at 46.8 pounds, the tabby died a relatively early death at age 10 from respiratory failure.

At the other extreme, was a Blue Point Himalayan named Tinker Toy who was a dwarf cat, meaning he suffered from a poorly understood genetic defect similar to human dwarfism. At maturity, Tinker only stood 2.75 inches tall at the shoulder, was 7.5 inches long and weighed less than two pounds.

The largest cat breed is the Ragdoll; males typically weigh between 12 to 20 pounds and females between 10 to 15 pounds (whereas the average domestic cat is between 8 to 10 pounds).

The smallest cat breed is the Singapura with the males weighing about six pounds and the females about four.

Hair and body

Aside from weight, other signs of a healthy cat can be found upon close examination, particularly of the hair and body. Such an inspection is best performed as an act of petting, or even as if giving a well-deserved massage, because most cats do not like all parts of their bodies touched indiscriminately. But do take a close look at your cat, get familiar with all body parts so you will know the difference immediately if health is beginning to decline in any area. Be sure to look at the following:

Ears

Did you realize a cat's hearing is much more sensitive than both a human's and dog's? To keep ears in prime condition to hear a cricket walking through the grass, they must be clean on the inside with no waxy residue, no brown or black secretions suggesting a mite problem, and no odor. Healthy ears are pink on the inside, and unless your cat is a Scottish fold, whose ear tips naturally fold down, they should be perky, pointed upright, and able to pivot a full 180 degrees.

Eyes

Eyes will be clear and bright with no evidence of chronic tearing or discharge. The third eyelid, the nictitating membrane that protects the eyes and helps keep them moist, will not be noticeable. Cats happen to have the largest eye of all mammals and are better adapted to see at night than humans. In fact, it is estimated they can see six times better in the dark than people can. Their night vision is superb because of the way their eyes are built — the muscles around the pupil allow it to change from a slit in bright light to nearly the full iris in dark, and there is a reflective layer behind the retina that works as a built-in flashlight by reflecting incoming light. Should you discover your cat seems to have difficulty seeing in the dark, or that the pupils are of different sizes, he or she may be suffering from vision problems.

The nose knows

Each cat nose is unique. The nose pad has ridges and patterns, like a human's fingerprint, that is distinguishable from every other cat on the planet.

Teeth

Adult cats have 30 teeth with 16 on the top and 14 on the bottom. You may already know this, but it bears repeating — be very careful when you examine your cat's teeth. He or she may be so upset by it that you will find out just how strong and sharp they are once they are impaled into your hand. Healthy teeth are white and sharp. Gums should be pink and shiny. Cats are prone to plaque and tartar buildup, but healthy cats — ones who have the opportunity for getting their teeth clean — will have none. Plaque will make teeth look yellow, and tartar will be even darker. Other signs to look for are cracked or broken teeth and breath odors. If kitty has a foul odor coming from its mouth, it may be indicative of gum disease or infection.

Hair

A cat's back holds approximately 60,000 hairs per square inch, which sounds like a lot until you realize the underside holds double that number. Cats have three types of hair. Guard hairs determine the coat color. These hairs help your cat stay dry, as they tend to repel water. Awn hairs are finer, softer hairs that form the basic coat, which grows under the guard hair. In most breeds, the awn hairs are the same length as the guard hair, but in some, like the Manx, these hairs are shorter. The undercoat hair is also called the "down" hair. It is the softest, fluffiest of the three types and provides warmth to your cat. It is also the hair that generally gets matted if a cat is not groomed frequently enough. A healthy cat's coat is soft and smooth. There are no bald patches or irregularities in the texture. It should come off when gently rubbed against sofas and trouser legs, but not in large tufts or with any sign of bleeding.

Skin

For most cats, the skin beneath the hair should be white. However, some have darker tones. Regardless of the color, healthy skin is smooth and taut. Evidence of potential problems includes scaly flakes, raised discolorations, and lesions. There should be no lumps under the skin or large red patches on it. You should not see any black specks or tiny particles that could be indicative of a flea infestation.

Movement and behavior

Appearances aside, healthy cats likes to show off their hale and hearty self. There is robustness when they pounce down off the back of a chair to attack your toes. They will strut with a confident gait across the room to bless you by rubbing against your legs. Or, with an accuracy that would awe a pool shark, they will attack the tail end of a scarf as it is being wrapped around an unsuspecting neck. A healthy cat just exudes confidence and coolness.

Though most adult cats are relatively calm, cool, and collected, kittens should be rather rambunctious. A healthy kitten is actively curious, eager to search every nook and cranny and discover what can move, can be moved, and what sounds those items make when they crash to the floor. Therefore, it also has the reflexes to make it jump out of the way or to leave the premises before any humans lumber up to discover the mess. If a kitten is in poor health, it is more apt to be lethargic. Curiosity will be fulfilled with a watchful gaze, and lengthy rests more befitting an older cat will follow the short spurts of energy.

As much as it seems like cats are always on the prowl or manage to stay in the way, healthy cats actually sleep quite a bit of the time. A mature, healthy adult cat will nap, on average, anywhere from 13 to 16 hours a day. Kittens will sleep even more than that. But if it seems your tabby is sleeping more than 16 hours, it could be a sign he or she is not getting enough energy from food or is fighting an illness. Stay on top of your cat's sleep patterns so you can easily spot changes.

Regardless of age, a healthy cat has a keen sense of balance. Cats have more bones in their bodies than humans do (people have about 206, compared to about 230 for cats, with the majority of their bones in the tail), and yet they have much better coordination and control of those bones than humans do. Cat owners hold their breath as their pets saunter along the outside edge of a stairwell or perch atop a fence post, seemingly aloof and unaware of their super-yoga feats. The tail is the cat's primary tool for keeping balance, but a supple body, fine-tuned central nervous system and highly evolved inner ear assist it. Those body parts all combine to give cats their innate sense of balance and poise. However, those super powers can suffer from malnutrition and show up in an unhealthy cat that has difficulty judging distances, whose coordination is wobbly, and who consistently suffers the aches and pains that arise from falling.

A healthy cat also has a graceful walk. Oddly, cats share their particular style of walking — taking a step with both their left feet and then the next step with both their right feet — with camels and giraffes, who do not share in the repute of style and elegance. It is assumed that such a gait increases the ability to be agile while silent. However, cats suffering from motor skill coordination problems may walk differently, as will cats with injured spinal columns or other painful conditions.

A final sign of healthy cat behavior is no tendency to engage in repetitive behaviors, such as head shaking or constant scratching. Similarly, healthy cats neither groom excessively nor completely forgo self-cleaning. If your cat engages in any repetitive or compulsive behavior, be sure to have him or her examined by a veterinarian, as it could be a sign of a serious health complication. Likewise, if your cat's behavior and movement does not fit with the healthy descriptions above, discuss with the veterinarian. There may just be an underlying health condition that you do not know about.

Homing instincts

Healthy cats have amazing homing instincts that enable them to find their way back home or to their beloved owners.

First, they have the ability to return home after being removed from it — even when removed and put into a maze to confuse them. Some scientists believe cats have an incredible sensitivity to the earth's magnetic field, as if they have some sort of internal compass that helps them find their way back home. A study tested this claim by attaching magnets to cats, and their homing abilities were impaired.

Cats also have what Dr. Joseph Rhine of Duke University refers to as a "psi trailing" ability — that is they are able to find their owners when they become separated. A famous example is when a veterinarian moved from New York to California and left his cat behind. The cat managed to track him down, find his new home, and plop himself into his old favorite chair. The veterinarian took X-rays to be certain, as his cat had an abnormality you could only see on X-ray film, and sure enough, it was his cat. The only theory out there to explain this ability, suggests that the cats that do this have formed an intense bond at the cellular level with their owners that allows them to sense where their humans are.

Your Cat's Natural Diet

It is believed that most domestic cats are descendants of small wild African cats living on or near a desert-like environment. Interestingly, there remain two species of wild cats — one in Europe called the forest wild cat and one in Africa, the desert cat — that are of similar size to domestic pets and continue to hunt in the wild today. Like the modern wild cats and the feral toms and tabbies found in alleyways and behind buildings, the ancestors of your pet cat lived off whatever food they could find — mainly birds, rodents, and other small mammals. Their typical diet — while all natural — may reflect more of what was currently available in the environment at that time, than what is best and most nutritionally sound for a cat. So, you cannot base all of your cat's meals on what feral or wild cats do. You can, however, certainly use their innate choices and behaviors as guidelines. For example, a feral cat's diet consists largely of wild mice whose body composition are roughly 60 percent protein, 30 percent fat, and the remaining 10 percent fiber and carbohydrates. That ratio is ideal for the foods you should feed your modern, domestic cats. You can use that ratio as a template upon which to base the meals you prepare for your pets.

Protein

Like their feral cousins and wild ancestors, our domestic cats are true carnivores. It is evident in the way their bodies are made to hunt. Their claws are designed to tear open flesh. Their long, sharp teeth are perfect for ripping through meat. Their keen hearing and vision are adapted for night hunting. And they have amazing ability to stalk — in perfect silence — your fuzzy slippers shuffling across the kitchen floor.

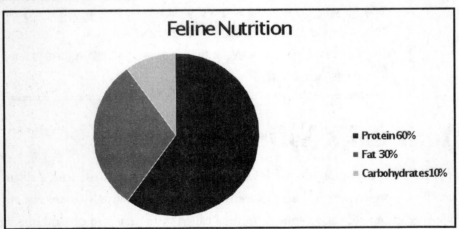

Aside from its undeniable hunting abilities, a cat's body is primed for digesting and processing the protein found in meat better than it can any other food source. When food enters a cat's mouth, it is attacked by protease, a digestive enzyme that specifically targets proteins in animal meats. Cat saliva is loaded with an abundance of protease, which breaks down protein, making it digestible so the body can absorb the nutrition in the meat. But the protease in saliva is only the beginning. The entire gastrointestinal system of a cat is primed for digesting and assimilating protein.

After the food leaves the cat's mouth and travels down into the stomach, the digestion process is continued by pepsin and lipase, more digestive enzymes that break the protein down into large nutrient molecules. Once the food travels out of the stomach and enters the cat's rather short intestines, even more protein-attacking enzymes go to work. Those enzymes are specifically designed to break the larger molecules down into smaller ones that can then be absorbed into the blood stream. At the molecular level, the blood throughout the cat's body will now distribute the amino acids that came from the protein. Some of those amino acids will then go to work creating and repairing muscle and tissue, and others will get converted into energy. After all, your cat does more than just lie in the sun looking beautiful and needs energy to stalk the broom and attack the toilet paper.

None of the protein in meat goes to waste in a cat. In truth, a cat's need for protein is greater than any other need for a nutrient or food component. The protein requirement is seconded only by fat, with carbohydrates at a distant third. In general, your cat's ideal diet is almost exclusively animal products with just a minimum of non-protein-based plant material. When aiming toward providing all the food in your cat's diet, your goal should reflect her needs and be: 55 to 60 percent protein, 25 to 30 percent fat, and 5 to 10 percent carbohydrates, which is just what a mouse would offer a wild or feral tabby.

Protein happens to be the only source of amino acids, which, as just mentioned, are necessary for building and repairing muscle tissue. They are also important for energy metabolism and other bodily functions. Amino acids are so integral to an animal's health that no carnivore or omnivore can live without them. In fact, some amino acids are so crucial in a cat's diet; they are called essential amino acids. In particular, a cat needs the essential amino acids arginine and taurine to be abundant in its diet. And, in yet another sign that cats are meant to eat meat, those amino acids are found in meat proteins only, not in grain or vegetable proteins.

- **Arginine:** Arginine assists with the removal of ammonia from a cat's body. When a protein reaches the gastrointestinal track of a cat, by-products and waste are created that will then need to be eliminated from the body. One of those by-products is ammonia. If ammonia is left to build up in your cat's body, it can create urinary stones, urinary tract infections, and other health issues. The job of arginine in the meat is to bind up the ammonia, making it possible for her to pass it out into her litter box. Many cat parents have noticed the odor of ammonia around the litter box or when their cat sprayed an area with urine to mark its territory. It is natural to have some ammonia odor on occasion, but if you are noticing it with increasing frequency or intensity, you may need to speak to your cat's veterinarian, as it could be a sign of a health issue. Arginine is so important in a cat's diet that without it, the ammonia will build up in her blood stream and reach toxic levels. It can then make her depressed, and if the levels continue to climb, she may even suffer from seizures.

- **Taurine:** Taurine is another essential amino acid for cats. In fact, cats need taurine more than any other animal does. Without adequate amounts of taurine, your cat could suffer from a whole host of disorders and diseases. They can go blind, deaf, or both. Their hearts will be affected; they will increase their odds of developing cardiomyopathy (a disease of the heart muscle) and heart failure. Their immune systems will weaken, making them more susceptible to viral and bacterial infections. Female cats can suffer from reproductive failure, and kittens will have slower growth, poor development, and possibly even congenital defects. Because of the necessity of your cat getting enough taurine in its diet, you will notice that many of the recipes in this book have taurine added to them, as you cannot give her too much.

Your cat's need for taurine suggests that at least one area where you should mimic wild cats is in ensuring that the protein portion of your domestic tabby's food comes from the whole animal, not just the muscle meat like humans generally consume. Taurine is not found in much muscle meat, but there are large amounts in the organ meats, such as the liver of beef and in the hearts, gizzards, liver, and dark meat of chicken and turkey. Wild or feral cats eat those organ meats every time they catch their prey. To be sure your cat gets enough taurine, you will either need to ensure an adequate supply of the nutrient in her foods or to give it to her in supplement form. Because taurine plays such an integral role in cat health it is now sold in both powder and capsule supplement form at most pet supply stores and natural health grocers.

When it comes to protein, cats digest chicken, lamb, turkey, and rabbit best. Many have problems breaking down pork, and some just do not like beef. And fish, while it can seem like it is your cat's favorite, should be kept to a minimum. Fish often releases a high amount of histamines in cats. Histamines are chemicals the immune system produces that cause inflammation and other allergic reaction symptoms, such as scabby, itchy skin, and itchy ears. If you know your cat is not allergic to fish, you may give it as a special treat maybe once or twice a week. However, be aware that even if your cat is not allergic to it, too much can lead to nutrient deficiencies because fish does not contain taurine and other essential amino acids. Aside from the potential health issues, fish seems to have an addictive quality to it. The reason is unknown, but cats fed fish on a regular basis often refuse to eat other forms of meat and become more finicky than usual.

Eggs, on the other hand, are an excellent source of protein for your cat. But you must serve them cooked because there is greater risk of bacterial infections from raw eggs. You must also use both the yolk and white parts of the egg. The white has the protein, and the yolk has the fat and other nutrients. Both parts are easily digestible, and cats seem to enjoy them equally. One large egg provides about six grams of protein, which is a little more than an ounce of chicken, beef, fish, or other animal proteins. You can feed your cat eggs every day as long as this is not the only source of protein you provide her. If you do follow this regimen, be sure to supplement the eggs with essential amino acids and a variety of healthy carbohydrates, which will be discussed later in this chapter.

Plant Protein

When humans become vegetarians, they learn how to fulfill their bodies' need for protein via plant matter. Soy, wheat gluten, corn, nuts, rice, and beans are all plants that contain good sources of protein. However, they are only good sources of protein for humans and not for cats for a couple of reasons:

1. Your cat cannot digest grains very well. Wheat and corn will cause her intestinal distress if you rely on it to fulfill her protein requirements.

2. None of the plant proteins contain arginine or taurine, the key essential amino acids for your cat's health. Cats are carnivores. Nature has created the perfect protein sources for their health in the animal species they eat.

Fat

Just like protein, the 25 to 30 percent of your cat's diet that consists of dietary fat should also come from animal sources. As you will learn in the section on carbohydrates, a cat's digestive system is just not developed to handle grains and grain products. Adding corn oil or soy oil to your cat's food as the primary source of fat can potentially cause your cat discomfort.

Though cats get a good portion of their energy from protein, they also get a fair amount from fat. Calorie counts are the same for humans as they are for cats. So, for each gram of protein or carbohydrate ingested, your cat receives four calories to burn off. For each gram of fat eaten, he or she receives nine calories to burn. The extra energy is good for cats that are highly active, but if these calories are not burned off, your cat's liver will very efficiently store it as fat. Some fat is necessary, but if you allow more than 30 percent of the diet to come from fat without enough exercise to burn it off, it will lead to obesity.

Fat gives your cat more than just energy. Similar to how amino acids are found in proteins, there are essential fatty acids in fats. Fatty acids are produced when the body breaks down ingested fat. They help oxygen move through the bloodstream. They are necessary for building cell walls and for overall cell health by helping stave off inflammation. They also help transport fat-soluble vitamins such as vitamins A, D, E, and K, which are needed for good eyesight, healthy bone structure, immune strength, and blood clotting. Additionally, appropriate amounts of essential fatty acids are what keep your cat's fur shiny and soft and his skin supple and taut.

Cats that do not get enough fat in their diets are at risk of suffering from a deficiency of essential fatty acids. The first signs of fatty acid deficiencies are often cosmetic. The hair will grow dull and thin, and the skin will become scaly and itchy. Continued deficiencies will start causing problems. Your cat will suffer from vision problems, central nervous system irregularities, and an impaired learning ability among a host of other poor health issues.

Good sources of fat come from the animals that give our cats good protein: the fat from chicken and other fowl, rabbits, beef suet, or small amounts of cold-water fish oil. Lard is not usually a healthy source of fat for cats because, although lard is animal based, it often contains a chemical called butylated hydroxyanisole (BHA), which is used as a preservative. BHA is linked to several health problems in animals including dry skin, allergic reactions, and dental disease. Studies have also shown BHA promotes liver disease and other, more serious, medical problems in many animals. As reported in *The Oxidative Enzymes in Foods*, studies on BHA conducted by J.K. Donnelly and D.S. Robinson showed an increase in liver fat coinciding with a decrease in liver muscle in animals given that preservative. Fatty liver is a specific health condition that can seriously harm and even kill your cat. *This will be discussed in Chapter 6.* It is imperative that you do not feed your cat any foods containing BHA.

Once you start shopping for natural foods for your cat, talk to the butcher at your local market about your need for quality meats and fats for your cat. You may just find yourself the happy recipient of fresh fat that must be cut off of the meats the grocer sells to human shoppers. Most butchers are happy to find a good home for those meat products to keep them from going to waste.

Carbohydrates

Carbohydrates supply some vital nutrients and fiber that cats need. However, cats can have a very difficult time digesting carbohydrate-laden foods. As mentioned in the discussion about protein, an assortment of digestive enzymes is produced in the bodies of humans, cats, and all other animals to help breakdown and digest food. Various enzymes target specific foods at particular points of digestion, and each species is engineered to produce differing amounts of individual enzymes that are tailored to the animal's diet. For example, one of the things that make cats carnivorous is the lack of amylase in their saliva, and they have low levels in their pancreas. Amylase is a digestive enzyme that targets carbohydrates and breaks them down to their molecular level, making them digestible. On the other hand, as mentioned previously, cats have large amounts of protease, which is geared toward breaking down protein.

If you observe cats in the wild, you will find they get their carbohydrates already partially digested by consuming the stomach contents of their prey, which usually contains grasses and other vegetation. Because their prey are often herbivores, those animals have the necessary enzymes to process the carbohydrates. By the time a cat hunts down the prey, the vegetation is already partially digested, which makes it easy for the cat to finish digesting it. Even if you wanted to, which you probably do not, it would be next to impossible for you to recreate such conditions in your home. Instead, to help your furry friend in your kitchen, you will need to offer her carbohydrates that are easily broken down — such as rice, boiled skinless potatoes, and vegetables. Finely chopping your vegetables and other carbohydrate sources will also make them easier for your cat to digest. To make it even easier on your cat's system, grind them in a food processor, or use the pulp left over after juicing them. Of course, if you grind your cat's meat, you can add vegetables in during the meat-grinding process.

The inability to properly digest carbohydrates is just one reason why you should limit them for your cat. Another reason is because many cats have allergies to carbohydrate grains, particularly to wheat, corn, soy, and yeast. Those sensitivities can exist on a barely noticeable level for a long time before they eventually cause your cat to suffer from serious conditions, such as inflammatory bowel disease. High levels of carbohydrates in a cat's diet also increase the odds of developing problems related to obesity and feline diabetes, and too many carbohydrates will upset the pH balance in a cat's urine, making the urine too alkaline. *The need for acidic urine is explained and discussed further in the section on feline urinary tract disease in Chapter 7.* But in essence, each animal has a unique pH balance to its body and urine. A cat's urine pH level must remain acidic for its urinary tract to remain healthy. Alkaline urine in a cat will create crystals, stones, and other urinary tract problems.

With all the negative issues associated with carbohydrates in a cat's diet, you may feel like you should just skip out on feeding any to your cat. It certainly would make meal preparation a little easier, but it would also lead to a very unhealthy cat. Though cats cannot thrive on a vegetarian diet, they cannot achieve their utmost health without at least some carbohydrates in their food. Carbohydrates provide fiber and essential vitamins and minerals a cat can only get from foods derived from plants that they cannot get from meat sources.

Fiber is necessary for stomach, intestine, and colon health. It helps keep stool the right consistency, therefore keeping trips to the litter box more pleasant. Fiber assists with the passage of items that are difficult to digest, including hair balls. Dietary fiber is also good for cats that are diabetic or overweight because, similar to the way fiber helps cat owners control their blood sugar, fiber helps manage glucose levels in cats as well. Cats that suffer from anal sac disease, chronic kidney disease, irritable bowel syndrome, colitis, or megacolon can also benefit from fiber. *See Chapter 6 for a discussion of each.* Those health issues are often caused by irritation or inflammation that results from inadequately digested food. Fiber in a cat's diet has a pacifying effect on all gastrointestinal functions, meaning it encourages proper digestion, eases the passing of wastes, and helps keep the tract clean, therefore creating less inflammation and irritation. Good sources of fiber for your cat's meals include rice bran, rice, whole oats, canned pumpkin, beets, carrots, and celery.

Yes, fiber is a good thing; but, as with all good things, too much can become a bad thing. An excessive amount of fiber in your cat's diet can create its own set of problems. If you feed your cat too much fiber, it may interfere with her ability to absorb particular nutrients. It can cause both constipation and diarrhea, and it can lead to anal fissures. So, be sure to keep it within the limits of the carbohydrates ratio in your cat's diet, which is 5 to 10 percent of each complete meal, regardless of the number of times you feed him or her each day.

What about fruit?

There really is no need to give your cat fruit. Not only will fruit make the cat's urine more alkaline, some fruit, such as citrus fruit and grapes, can make a cat very sick. Besides, cats do not even enjoy a sweet taste, as they lack the sweet receptor gene. It is best to just stay away from fruit when preparing meals for your cats

To help extract the vital nutrients found only in vegetables and other plant foods, domestic cats have evolved longer intestines than their wild counterparts, which helps slow down the processing of food just enough to make it easier on them to eat vegetation. In addition to the fiber sources mentioned above, your cat can benefit from the nutrients in pumpkin, peas, and green leafy vegetables. There is a more complete list at the end of this chapter to help you decide which vegetables are good for your cat.

At the beginning stages of switching your cat over to a home-cooked or all-natural diet, you will need to be on high alert to see if he or she is having difficulty with any particular carbohydrates. Though it is safe to say that most cats simply cannot process corn, wheat, or soy, it is not so easy to make such sweeping generalizations about other carbohydrates. For example, some cats can tolerate and even enjoy spinach quite nicely, while others will suffer gas pains. Take some time to learn which carbohydrates your cat likes and tolerates as you add them to the diet.

Moisture

In addition to protein, fat, and carbohydrates, there is a fourth component to a healthy diet for cats — moisture. In the wild, cats obtain their moisture from the animals they catch, whose bodies are up to 75 percent water. As it is with pet owners, water is imperative for good health in cats. Water helps regulate a cat's body temperature, preventing it from suffering from both heat exhaustion and hyperthermia. It helps in the digestion of food and in the elimination of wastes. Water lubricates tissues, keeping them supple and strong. It also serves as the medium that salt and other electrolytes use to pass through the cat's body.

When creating meals and treats for your cat, you need to keep the moisture content in mind. Cats should never eat completely dry food. Urinary tract problems and kidney failure in cats have been closely related to a lack of water. According to Michael R. Lappin's *Feline Internal Medicine Secrets*, proper hydration — that is, maintaining adequate levels of water in your cat's body — is crucial for kidney and urinary tract performance and health. Therefore, it is best for your cat to eat food that has water added to it, unless it is naturally moist. If your cat loves kibble, be sure he or she has a bowl of fresh water nearby, and monitor it to ensure he or she is drinking frequently as he eats his dry food.

Your cat's keen sense of smell may enable him or her to notice chlorine or other chemicals or minerals that may be unpleasant in your tap water. So, do not let yourself be fooled into thinking your cat is getting enough water because he or she is not drinking it. If you feed your cat kibble on a regular basis and he or she is snubbing the water, try offering some spring water from a bottle or water that has had all the impurities filtered out of it. It is very possible your cat will only drink water that smells "cleaner."

You may have noticed that milk and dairy products were not mentioned in the sections on protein and fat, and perhaps you are expecting to read about them here. After all, cats love milk, right? Everyone has seen adorable kittens lapping up bowls of milk, but that does not mean it is a good idea to give dairy products to your cats. Most cats are actually lactose intolerant, meaning they lack the digestive enzymes to properly digest milk and milk products. Because their bodies can take so long trying to digest the lactose in milk, dairy products wind up staying in the intestinal tract too long — long enough to ferment. The cat will then suffer from gas, cramps, diarrhea, and other discomforts.

If you know for sure that your cat likes and tolerates dairy products, you can give him or her a special treat once or twice a week. Using full-fat products, such as heavy cream or whole milk, will be best because the more fat there is in the food, the less lactose there will be. If your cat absolutely loves milk, but you know he or she cannot tolerate it, you could also try lactose-free milk found at your local grocer. Often, it works well, as does Greek yogurt or goat's milk yogurt.

Yes, water is the primary source of hydration in your cat's food, but as you continue through this book and contemplate what changes you want to make in your cat's diet, you will notice that how you supply water to your cat will have a great influence over the rest of the diet. For example, if you decide to feed your cat a raw-foods diet, as discussed in Chapter 4, you will not need to worry whether or not he or she is getting enough liquids because the animal products you will be feeding him or her will have adequate levels of moisture in them. Otherwise, if you decide to cook for your cat, you may find you will need to add water or meat-based broths to the finished food.

Kitty want a cocktail?

Harry was a cat Linda Wilt, a writer from Ohio, had when she was a child. He was a classic, tuxedo-style black and white, shorthaired cat, with coincidentally, olive-green eyes. Harry was several years old when the family realized he was crazy about green olives. One evening Wilt was preparing a casserole for dinner, and the recipe called for green olives stuffed with pimento. Before Wilt knew what was happening, Harry jumped up onto the counter and stuck his head into the open jar of olives. She shoved him off, onto the floor, but it was like he was on springs. He jumped right back up and stuck his head back into the jar. After that, Wilt would toss him an olive every once in a while for a treat, and he would always roll all over it on the floor before he carried it off to eat it.

One year, Wilt's father went to Israel with a group of Presbyterian ministers, and brought back hand-carved olive wood Christmas tree ornaments as gifts. No one realized Harry might just have a penchant for them. When the tree was put up, he snuck one off a low branch. The family found it later, gnawed and drooled over behind the couch, with some pieces missing. Apparently, Harry's olive addiction got the better of him. After that, the family kept those ornaments higher on the tree.

Cat Friendly Foods

In short, the following table shows the best foods you can feed your cat to meet requirements for protein, fat, and carbohydrates. Many will be found in your local market, but others, particularly some of the protein suggestions, may only be found at farms or pet specialty stores. The convenience of finding food for your cat next to your own is a nice bonus, but after you start preparing meals for your purring companions, you might just find you are tempted to go the extra step and find them specialty meats.

Protein and fat sources	Carbohydrate sources
Cornish game hen	Carrots
Turkey	Pumpkins
Chicken	Sweet potatoes
Beef (lean)	Winter squash (acorn and butternut)
Buffalo	Summer squash, zucchini

Bison	Celery
Ostrich	Parsnips
Venison	Peas
Emu	Green beans
Lamb	Greens (dandelion, collards, kale, Swiss chard)
Elk	Grasses (wheat, rye, oat, barley)
Fish (1 to 2 times a week)	Rice bran
Whole-fat milk products (if your cat tolerates it)	White skinless cooked potatoes
Whole cooked eggs	
Guinea fowl	
Rabbit	
Quail	
Mice	
Vole	
Gopher	
Pheasant	

Specific nutrient needs

If you feed your cat a variety of the above foods in the proper ratios (protein 55 to 60 percent, fat 25 to 30 percent, and carbohydrates 5 to 10 percent of total calories), you will provide him or her with the basic four needs: protein, fat, carbohydrates, and moisture. Most nutritional needs will be met as well, but you must remain aware that cats have specific vitamin and mineral requirements that you will need to cater to.

Minerals

Cats, like their human owners, need a variety of nutritional minerals if they are to achieve and maintain good health. Most minerals are naturally present in foods, and by following the protein-fat-carbohydrate ratio mentioned above, you will find an easy way to make sure your cat gets the variety of minerals needed. But it is not enough just to be sure your cat is getting the right kind of minerals in his or her diet. You will also need to be mindful of how much of each she is getting. Too much of a particular mineral, as well as an inadequate supply of it, can lead to disease and other serious health complications. You need to be aware of the potential problems that both an excessive or toxic amount and a deficient amount of certain minerals may cause.

- **Calcium:** Calcium helps form and maintain the health and strength of bone and teeth. It enables muscles, including the heart, to contract, and it assists in blood clotting and nerve impulse transmission. Too much calcium will stunt a kitten's growth, make an older cat's bones too dense, and may decrease appetite. Too little of the mineral will lead to a weakened skeleton, which can easily lead to broken bones or a collapsed spine.

  In the wild, cats eat the bones of their prey to get their calcium requirements, but it can be problematic to feed your domestic cat animal bones. Once bones are cooked, they become brittle and easily breakable. If your cat should eat a cooked bone, he or she risks getting a piece of bone puncturing an internal organ, lacerating the esophagus and blocking the intestines, which would require surgery to remove the stuck bone. Therefore, unless you will be feeding your kitty raw meats, where you can grind up the bones into the food, you will need to provide other sources of calcium for your cat.

  - *Eggshell powder:* An easily found source of calcium is eggshell powder. You can buy it in natural foods and pet food stores, but you can also make it at home yourself with your leftover eggshells. *See the Supplement Section of the Recipes in Chapter 9 of this book for directions on creating your own eggshell powder.*

  - *Bone meal:* Along with calcium, bone meal contains a host of other trace essential minerals. As its name implies, bone meal consists of crushed and ground bones. Though it is an excellent source of calcium, you must be sure to find a pure, high-quality product because in the 1980s, many bone meal supplements were found to contain lead and other toxic heavy metals. Then, in the 1990s, the fear of bovine spongiform encephalopathy (more popularly referred to as mad cow disease) became another concern. You can still find bone meal in health food stores, and some natural pet supply stores carry it as well. If you choose to use it, check the label to determine how it was quality checked for safety.

- *Calcium carbonate:* Another supplement you can purchase at a health food market or pet supply store is calcium carbonate. It is actually the calcium found in eggshells. It is also naturally present in many rocks, shellfish, shells, and pearls. However, you can simply purchase it in capsule form as a supplement.

- *Vegetables:* Non-animal sources of calcium include vegetable greens, in particular, Swiss chard, collard greens, dandelion greens, kale, mustard greens, and parsley, which happen to be vegetables that are safe for your cat to consume. However, a serving of these vegetables for your cat will be smaller than a tablespoon, and will not contain enough calcium for his or her daily supply. Therefore, vegetable sources should be considered only as an adjunct to your main source.

- *Dairy:* Of course, if you know for sure your cat handles dairy without any adverse issues, whole-fat milk products offer another source of calcium. Yogurt and cottage cheese seem to be a favorite among some cats. Others happily lap up ground Parmesan cheese sprinkled over their moist food.

Orphaned kittens can often tolerate and benefit by getting the good nutrition offered from goat's milk yogurt. But remember, feeding your cat dairy products really should be kept to a minimum of a couple times a week as it will also fulfill a protein portion of your cat's diet without providing the essential amino acids that meat products do.

- **Magnesium:** Magnesium assists with the ever-important enzyme functions in a cat's body. It strengthens nerve- and muscle-cell membranes and aids hormone secretion. Magnesium works in conjunction with calcium, assisting in the building of mineral structure of bones and teeth. Where calcium is necessary for muscle contraction; magnesium is necessary for muscle relaxation. The two work together with all muscles, including the heart, which beats by contracting and relaxing.

  Not enough magnesium will result in poor growth in kittens or muscle twitching and convulsions in older cats. Good sources for magnesium are also good sources for easily digested carbohydrates, such as: pumpkins, pumpkin seeds, and the leafy green vegetable Swiss chard. Protein sources are halibut, salmon, and Chinook fish.

- **Phosphorous:** Phosphorous is another mineral that works hand-in-hand with calcium on the cat's skeleton. It is also necessary for DNA structural health, energy metabolism, and cat movement. Cats deficient in phosphorous suffer from locomotor disturbances where they become unable to properly control their physical movements. Phosphorous deficiency is also linked to a specific form of anemia. Phosphorous toxicity is seldom a problem, however, cats suffering from chronic renal failure should limit their phosphorous intake, otherwise it will exacerbate the problem. Good sources include meat, dairy, and fish.

- **Potassium:** Potassium is necessary for cats to maintain their pH acid/alkaline levels, for proper fluid balance, and to assist with nerve impulse processes. Deficient or excessive potassium is difficult for cats to achieve, therefore, not a concern.

- **Sodium and chlorine:** These two minerals are similar to potassium and are necessary for maintaining fluid levels and proper acid/alkaline balance in the body. Chlorine also assists the cat's stomach in making hydrochloric acid, which helps digest protein. Sodium helps transport nutrients into cells and then removes waste from them. Sodium and chlorine are found in just about all foods, so deficiencies are rare. And if cats have easy access to drinking water or enough moisture in their foods so their bodies can expel those minerals, toxicity is also rare. An excess of sodium or chlorine in a cat shows up as extreme thirst, anorexia, stunted growth, and excessive urination.

- **Iron:** Iron is important for healthy blood and energy metabolism. Too much iron in your cat's diet will lead to vomiting and diarrhea, and too little will cause slow growth, weakness, and lethargy. Excellent sources for iron are meats and dark green vegetables, such as kale and Swiss chard.

- **Copper:** Copper is necessary for muscle and organ tissue health, blood cell creation, and overall cell health. Copper deficiencies, while rare in cats, do show up with symptoms such as weight reduction and anemia. In growing kittens, symptoms of copper deficiency include bone deformities and abnormalities. Too much copper, or copper toxicity, is generally not a problem in cats as it is present in most foods in tiny or trace amounts, which is all your cat needs. Good sources for copper include liver and fish, two of their favorite foods. Just remember, fish should be saved for special treats and is not to be used as an everyday meal source.

- **Zinc:** Proper levels of zinc in your cat's system will benefit the coat and skin. Zinc also assists with cell reproduction, wound healing, and energy metabolism. A zinc deficiency will manifest as skin lesions and slow growth. Toxic levels are extremely rare as, like copper, zinc is present in only trace amounts in foods. Zinc sources include meat, bone meal, fish, and rice.

- **Manganese:** Manganese is needed in very small quantities in cats, but it is used in very big ways. Manganese is necessary for proper bone development and neurological functioning. It is only found in small amounts in foods, so too much manganese is not a problem. Similarly, the need is so small for manganese that deficiency is not a concern. Good sources of manganese are eggs, pumpkin seeds, and green vegetables.

- **Selenium:** Selenium is vitamin E's partner when it comes to strengthening the immune system and fighting off oxidative damage to tissues. Selenium is readily available in most meat, including chicken and turkey, so deficiencies are almost unheard of in cats. It can also be found in rice, oats, and grains that are easily digested by cats. Excess amounts of selenium is equally rare because cats can usually handle what is supplied to them, but in the exceptional case in which it appears, cats suffer from hair loss, anemia, and even, in extreme cases, cirrhosis of the liver.

- **Iodine:** As with humans, cats need a sufficient supply of iodine for a healthy thyroid. The thyroid gland is responsible for maintaining your cat's energy metabolism. If it is underactive, the cat could suffer from hypothyroidism where she has less energy and is more prone to gaining weight. If it is overactive, the reverse is true: The cat will have an excessive amount of energy and difficulty keeping weight on. Iodine also assists with proper growth and development and helps regulate metabolism. Too much iodine will result in excessive tearing in the eyes, a nasal discharge, and dandruff. Too little will cause an enlarged thyroid gland. Iodine is found in fish and iodized salt.

Vitamins

Vitamins play crucial roles in cats' health just as they do for every living thing. A healthy cat needs a variety of vitamins to prevent a host of health problems. But, similar to minerals, too much of a particular vitamin will be toxic for your cat and can even lead to death. Again, the key to creating a balanced, healthy meal with proper amounts of key nutrients is in using a variety of foods. By using a diversity of ingredients, your cat will benefit by getting all of the vitamin nutrition she needs. An exact list of needed vitamins is too long to list here, and may not even be completely known or understood as researchers continue to discover vitamins in foods. The following list contains the key nutrients to be aware of when designing your favorite feline's menu.

- **Vitamin A:** The myth about carrots being good for your eyes has a hint of truth to it. Carrots are loaded with vitamin A, which is necessary for good vision, and because carrots are on the list of vegetables that are safe to feed your cat, they are a good source of vitamin A. Vitamin A is also crucial for growth and development and for a healthy immune system in your cat. However, too much vitamin A can cause skeletal lesions in kittens and osteoporosis in older cats. Too little of it will cause eye problems, such as conjunctivitis, night blindness, retinal degeneration, and cataracts. Vitamin A deficiency will also create muscle weakness, poor growth, and reproductive disorders. Sources of vitamin A, along with carrots, include liver, fish liver oil, dairy products, and green vegetables.

- **Vitamin D:** Proper mineral absorption and balance require adequate levels of vitamin D in your cat. This vitamin also helps maintain phosphorous balance and skeletal strength. Deficiencies lead to the bone-softening disease rickets, paralysis, weight loss, and skeletal deformities. Toxic levels will cause vomiting, lethargy, and anorexia. Sources of vitamin D include fortified dairy products (the label on the carton of milk or package of cheese will specifically state that it contains added vitamin D) and fish liver oil. The primary source of vitamin D for all animals is sunlight. So, while your tabby is reclined, squinting in a beam of sunlight, realize she is hard at work obtaining her recommended daily allowance of vitamin D.

- **Vitamin E:** This vitamin works with selenium to fight free radicals and prevent oxidative damage to tissues. Your cat really cannot get too much vitamin E, but if he or she does not get enough, your cat may develop anorexia, a sensitive stomach, and a condition called brown bowel syndrome, where your cat's bowels disintegrate and hemorrhage. Sources for vitamin E are meats and dark green leafy vegetables.

- **Vitamin K:** For blood to clot, cats (and humans) must get a sufficient amount of vitamin K. Too little may cause hemorrhaging. Sources of vitamin K are kelp and cooked egg yolk.

- **Vitamin B1:** This vitamin is also called thiamine. It is necessary for carbohydrates to metabolize into energy. Excessive or toxic amounts of thiamine is not usually a problem for cats, but a deficiency will cause seizures, loss of appetite, weight loss, heart rate disorders, and neurological impairments. Thiamine is found in all meat and dairy products and vegetables.

- **Vitamin B2:** This vitamin is also called riboflavin. It assists with enzyme functions in cats. Too little of this vitamin will cause fatty livers, eye problems, and heart failure. Riboflavin is found in dairy products and organ meats.

- **Vitamin B3:** Also known as niacin, B3 is necessary for enzymatic functioning. Too little niacin will cause extreme weight loss, elevated body temperature, and ulcers. It is found in most meats and meat by-products.

- **Vitamin B5:** Vitamin B5 is also called pantothenic acid. It assists with energy metabolism. The first sign of a deficiency is diarrhea. If the deficiency is not spotted and is allowed to continue, the cat will lose its hair. Toxicity of pantothenic acid in cats has not been reported.

- **Vitamin B6:** Vitamin B6's lesser-known name is pyridoxine. It plays a role in blood sugar creation, healthy red blood cells, proper nervous system functioning, hormone regulation, and immune response. A deficiency shows up as stunted growth, hair loss, or premature graying, seizures, and kidney problems. Getting vitamin B6 is easy, because it is found in most whole foods, including brown rice, whole oats, eggs, and beef. Processing foods will deplete the amount of vitamin B6 though, so be careful not to overcook them.

- **Vitamin B9:** Better known as folic acid, vitamin B9 metabolizes the amino acids found in proteins. It is also necessary for proper DNA synthesis. A lack of vitamin B9 will result in slowed growth, excessive iron in the blood, and bone marrow abnormalities. Vitamin B9 is easily stored in the cat's liver until it is needed, so issues relating to toxic levels of it are rarely a problem for cats.

- **Vitamin B12:** The other name for vitamin B12 is cyanocobalamin. Similar to riboflavin, vitamin B12, aids in the proper functioning of enzymes in a cat's body. Deficiencies of vitamin B12 will cause vomiting and diarrhea that will lead to excessive weight loss. Intestinal disorders will also manifest. Sources of B12 are meats — organ meats in particular. Your cat's body is adept at pulling out and using B12 from its food source, so deficiencies are not often reported. And, perhaps because it is not overly abundant, problems relating to toxic levels of this nutrient are very rarely experienced.

Supplements

If your tabby is an extra picky eater, you may need to consider supplements to be sure he or she is getting the needed nutrients to thrive. Some nutrients, such as the essential amino acid, taurine, might be a good idea to add to his or her meals regardless of the content in the food. As mentioned in the section on protein earlier in this chapter, taurine is vital for your cat, and she cannot get too much of it. But other nutrients, such as salt, may not be necessary at all if your cat is getting plenty of it naturally in food. When considering supplements for your cat's food, be sure to speak with your veterinarian to see if there are particular concerns for your cat that need to be addressed.

It is very difficult to find a definitive answer of how many grams or milligrams of a particular nutrient your cat needs. The Food and Drug Administration created a food pyramid for humans and determined recommended daily allowances of a variety of vitamins and minerals for human health. However, there really is no governing body doing the same for cats and their nutritional needs. The Board of Agriculture's Nutrient Requirements of Cats, Revised Edition, 1986 and the Association of American Feed Control Official's (AAFCO) Dog and Cat Food Nutrient Profiles provide recommendations to commercial pet food manufacturers detailing what they consider to be appropriate amounts of nutrients for cats. Unfortunately, their requirements are difficult to translate into an easily usable guideline for adding nutrients to your cat's home-cooked meals because the recommendations require a certain amount of grams of each nutrient to be added to each kilogram of packaged, dry food product. For example, the AAFCO requires 10.4 grams of arginine to be in each kilogram of dry, commercially prepared cat food. Because there are 1,000 grams in one kilogram, that means 1.04 percent of the meal is arginine. Now then, how is a human chef to ensure that much arginine is in the chicken for the cat?

Regardless, if you are feeding your cat a variety of meats and a diversity of carbohydrate sources, she is probably getting all the nutrition she needs. However, if she is a particularly finicky tabby, you may want to add in some crucial vitamins in safe amounts in supplement form. The following provides a guideline for adding common nutrients to your cat's food. The amount is based on use in a healthy cat, weighing between 8 and 10 pounds and eating around 250 calories per day. The units of measure reflect how the supplements are weighed, labeled, and sold: either mg for milligrams, or IU for international units. Again, be sure to check with your cat's veterinarian to be sure his or her needs are in alignment with this chart or if you need to make adjustments for your personal situation.

Vitamin A	500 IU
Vitamin B-complex:	10 mg
Vitamin C:	250 mg
Vitamin D:	50 IU

There are more supplements you may wish to incorporate into your cat's diet that depend on a variety of factors.

- **Taurine:** This should always be added to your cat's food. But how much is determined by how the food is prepared. If you are feeding your cat a raw foods diet, you will need to add 250 mg daily. However, if you are feeding her a cooked foods diet, you will want to up that amount to 500 mg daily if you are putting the taurine in prior to cooking.

- **Calcium:** If you decide to feed your cat an all-raw diet and include providing him or her with raw bones, you will probably not need to use a calcium supplement. However, if you are cooking the foods, you will need to use a supplement. You should try to give your cat 1,000 mg usable calcium every day. Usable calcium is the calcium your cat's body will be able to absorb from food. Not all the calcium in food is absorbable. For example, an easy source of calcium is ground eggshells. One eggshell will create about one teaspoon of eggshell powder, which has more than 5,000 mg of calcium in it. However, only about 1,800 mg of it will be usable. Other sources of calcium supplements include calcium carbonate powder (2,500 mg will provide 1,000 mg usable calcium) and calcium lactate (7,692 mg will provide 1,000 mg usable calcium).

- **Trace minerals:** The minerals that your cat needs in very small amounts are called trace minerals. They include magnesium, beryllium, bismuth, and chromium. They are almost impossible not to get from a diverse diet. However, again, for those very picky eaters, you may want to discuss with your cat's veterinarian if supplementing with trace minerals is a good option for your cat.

Another reason to discuss supplements with your veterinarian is that cautions must be taken with both vitamin A and vitamin D. Though both are necessary for your cat's health, too much is toxic. Both vitamins are easily stored in your cat's liver, unlike other vitamins that your cat will eliminate in waste. If the food you regularly feed your cat has vitamin A in it — chicken and beef liver, giblets, whole eggs, and oily fish — you do not need to add it as a supplement to your cat's food. On the other hand, muscle meat, such as chicken thighs or turkey breasts, is lacking in vitamin A, so you will need to be sure your cat also gets liver, other organs, or even bone meal to correct that deficiency.

If you do combine supplements with your cat's food, you may find it easier to incorporate the vitamins into the food if you grind them in a food processor along with the food you are preparing. Or, if the nutrient is oil based — like vitamin A, D, E, and K — you can poke a hole into the capsule and squirt the liquid over the food. A final word about vitamin and mineral supplements for your cat: Remember he or she is a carnivore. Be sure the supplements you mix in with the food are made from animal sources. Look on the label for fillers that may include dairy products and wheat or other grains he may be sensitive to, and never give him supplements made for a human. Humans have different nutritional needs than cats. What may be healthy, even necessary for humans, may be a lethal dose for your cat.

CASE STUDY: THE NECESSITY OF SUPPLEMENTS

Callie Novak, vice president
Dynamite Marketing
800-697-7434
www.dynamitemarketing.com

The ideal way to make homemade cat food — although impractical for most people — is to start by producing the meat yourself. For example, if you want to feed your cat poultry, you can raise chickens, and be certain that they eat a proper diet with all of the needed vitamins and minerals. The cat, in turn, will have all of the appropriate ingredients in its diet.

If you buy the meat for homemade cat food at the grocery store, it is impossible to know what the animals were fed. Your cat may be missing a number of nutrients.

An added vitamin and mineral supplement is a critical addition to homemade cat food, if you do not raise your own meat. Additionally, supplements are important for indoor cats, and even for outdoor cats that are not supplementing their diet regularly by hunting. Processed food (including commercially purchased meat), as opposed to freshly killed small animals, does not have the enzyme activity that cats require for proper digestion.

Cats have special nutritional requirements for elements that come only from animal sources, such as taurine. The amino acid, taurine, is necessary for good digestion of fats in the small intestine. Unlike many species, cats cannot use other amino acids for this function. Taurine is found only in animal ingredients.

One of the most common health problems in cats, probably right after skin and allergy problems, is urinary tract infections and disorders. These include struvite or oxalate stones and cystitis. Oxalate stones are caused by too much oxalic acid or oxalate and too little calcium in the diet. Struvite stones are a combination of magnesium, phosphate, and ammonium.

Dr. Lynn Peck, a holistic vet at the University of Florida, has referenced a study that demonstrates a link between low beneficial bacteria in the gut and oxalate stone formation. Fermentation extracts, or probiotics, have proven to be a big boost for cats with tendencies to develop stones and urinary tract infections. Dynamite Marketing recommends supplementing cat food, whether homemade or commercially purchased, with three products:

Purrformance (a probiotic and blend of vitamins), chelated minerals (taurine and other nutrients specifically designed for cats), and Liquid Purrformance (a combination of the other two). Dynamite Marketing is a family-owned business specializing in animal nutrition for four generations. The company uses only natural ingredients made in the United States for better quality control. Throughout its history, it has always looked at alternatives to animal by-products, antibiotics, chemical preservatives, fumigants, artificial coloring, and other additives that have later caused health problems. Its manufacturing processes are so stringently controlled that Dynamite has a separate mill to produce feed for herbivores, such as horses and poultry that are especially sensitive to contamination from meat needed by other species, such as dogs and cats.

Foods to Avoid

As you plan your cat's menu and learn to create meals that are both to his or her liking and health, you will need to keep in mind that there is a long list of foods a cat should never eat. They include:

- **Alcohol:** The cat liver is not able to detoxify alcohol; repeated ingestion can cause liver damage, comas, and lead to death.

- **Avocado:** Avocados contain persin, a fungicidal toxin that is harmless to humans but dangerous for cats. Avocados will really upset your cat's stomach, making him or her vomit and suffer from diarrhea. The toxin will also cause respiratory and heart issues in your cat that can eventually lead to death.

- **Baby food:** For some reason, there are cat parents who misguidedly feed their cats human baby foods, believing that because they are safe for babies they must be harmless to cats. Unfortunately, many baby foods have high carbohydrate content and are filled with wheat and soy, which your cat cannot tolerate well. Also, the meat-based baby foods often contain onion powder, which is toxic to cats.

- **Bones:** As mentioned in earlier in this chapter, cooked bones become brittle. If a cat should eat one, it can lacerate an intestine or become lodged inside him or her.

- **Canned tuna:** Fresh tuna is fine to feed your cat every once in a while, but canned tuna often contains high levels of mercury, which can cause neurological problems in your cat.

- **Chocolate and cocoa:** Theobromine is a substance in chocolate that will make a cat's heart have an irregular heartbeat and will also cause frequent urination. A cat that eats chocolate or cocoa may suffer initially with hyperactivity and excessive thirst. If your cat ingests a large enough amount, he or she may further suffer from vomiting, diarrhea, and even from heart attack.

- **Coffee and tea:** As with humans, caffeine will make your cat hyperactive and speed up his or her heart rate. Coffee and tea contains theobromine, which can cause vomiting and even be toxic for the heart.

- **Citrus and citrus oil extracts:** Citrus is extremely upsetting to a cat's stomach and may induce vomiting.

- **Dairy products**: Only feed your cat milk and other dairy products if you are absolutely certain he or she is not lactose intolerant. If your cat truly loves milk, you can offer lactose-free milk, goat's milk, and evaporated milk.

- **Dog food:** Canine treats and kibble may not cause a problem for your cat initially, but fed repeatedly may result in malnutrition and heart complications.

- **Fat trimmings:** Cats need fat for energy and essential fatty acids, but fat trimmings served alone can cause pancreatitis.

- **Garlic:** It is believed that most cats can tolerate garlic in small amounts that is less than an ounce a day, but larger amounts can be toxic. However, there are no studies to date specifying exactly how much is too much. There are few benefits to feeding your cat garlic, so unless your veterinarian suggests giving it to your cat for pest control or heart conditions, you may just want to leave it out of his or her food.

- **Grapes and raisins:** Cats cannot ingest grapes, raisins, or other grape products because even in tiny amounts, they can cause damage to a cat's kidneys.

- **Green tomatoes and tomato leaves:** Tomatoes, along with potatoes, are in the same plant family as the deadly nightshade. They contain a poisonous alkaloid, glycoalkaloid solanine, which a cat's sensitive stomach just cannot handle. Cooking ripe tomatoes will deplete all the glycoalkaloid solanine from them, but not from green tomatoes or the tomato plant.

- **Human vitamin supplements:** Cats' vitamin and mineral needs are very different from their owners'. Human vitamin supplements are toxic for a cat because they are geared toward an animal with different nutrient needs. Also, many human supplements contain wheat and soy products in them as filler.

- **Liver:** Though small amounts of liver is perfectly fine for a cat and is even a great source of the essential amino acid, taurine, large amounts of it will create vitamin A toxicity. If you want to serve your cat liver, you can mix it in with the other meat he or she is eating that day; feed tiny, teaspoon-sized amounts as a special treat, or just do not feed your cat liver every day.

- **Nuts:** Macadamia nuts in particular seem to be toxic to cats, but you should refrain from feeding your cat any kind of nuts. Most contain high levels of phosphorous, which although it is a needed mineral, can be toxic if a cat ingests too much.

- **Onions:** Onions were just not made for dogs and cats. Onions and all onion products contain disulfides that damage and destroy red blood cells and cause anemia.

- **Persimmons:** The seeds in persimmons can create blockages in your cat's intestines and cause the gastrointestinal infection enteritis.

- **Pork:** Most cats do not handle pork well; it seems to upset their stomachs.

- **Raw potatoes:** Although cooked, skinless white potatoes are fine for your cat, raw potatoes contain a poisonous substance called glycoalkaloid solanine that can create serious gastrointestinal upset. The uncooked peelings and green potatoes contain that substance as well and are equally toxic to your cat.

- **Rhubarb:** The leaves of rhubarb contain oxalates, which can be toxic and cause a condition called oxalic poisoning that will result in kidney failure. A cooked rhubarb stem is relatively safe for a cat to eat, but its fiber content is much too high to tolerate well.

- **Raw eggs:** Raw eggs not only carry a risk of salmonella poisoning, but they also contain avidin, an enzyme that will inhibit the cat's ability to absorb vitamins if eaten too often.

- **Raw fish:** Feeding your cat raw fish on a regular basis can lead to a vitamin B1, or thiamine deficiency. Some fish also contain parasites and such environmental pollutants as PCGs or mercury, which can weaken a cat's immune system.

- **Salt:** Depending on your cat's particular state of health, he or she may be able to have salt added to his food, but consult your veterinarian first, because too much salt will lead to an electrolyte imbalance.

- **Sugar:** A cat's body was not meant to ingest sugar. As in humans, sugar can lead to diabetes, obesity, and dental problems.

Other Potential Toxins

Cat owners must also be aware that the world is full of other items that are toxic and dangerous to their pets. Many houseplants, for example, can make your cat sick should he or she decide to nibble on one. Most cat owners give up on having houseplants, but a few are tenacious enough to keep trying even though their tabby is a green muncher. If you are a cat owner who continues to maintain houseplants, you must always avoid putting any plants found on the rather long list that follows in your home. And, because the amount of plants around the world is too numerous to catalogue, be aware that there may even be more. If you have any questions about whether or not a plant is safe to have around animals, research it thoroughly prior to bringing it into your home.

The plants on the next pages make up what seems like an all-encompassing list, but they are not the only potential toxins in your home. Your kitty may be attracted to the scents of household cleaners, which could make her sick. Even the "natural" cleaners can be a danger, because the key ingredients are often plant-based. And it may seem obvious, but it is so important it bears mentioning here, products created for use in your automobiles, such as antifreeze, gasoline, and windshield washing liquid will be lethal to your cat. Believe it or not, antifreeze has a scent to it that actually draws animals to it, so do not be complacent and think that your picky cat would not like it.

Aloe vera	Croton	Holly
Amaryllis	Corydalis	Honeysuckle
Arrowgrass	Crocus	Hurricane plant
Asparagus fern	Philodendron	Hyancinth
Azalea	Cycads	Hydrangea
Baby's breath	Cyclamen	Indian rubber plant
Belladonna	Daffodil	Iris
Bird of paradise	Datura	Lantana
Bittersweet	Devil's ivy	Larkspur
Bleeding heart	Delphinium	Lily
Bloodroot	Decentrea	Lily spider
Bluebonnet	Dieffenbachia	Lily of the valley
Boxwood	Dracaena	Lupine
Branching ivy	Dragon tree	Marigold
Buttercup	Dumb cane	Mistletoe
Cactus	Easter lilly	Mother-in-law's tongue (Sanseveria)
Caladium calla lilly	Elderberry	
Dieffenbachia	Elephant ear	
Chinese evergreen	Emerald feather	
Christmas rose	English ivy	
Chrysanthemum	Ferns	
Clematis	Geranium	
Dordatum	German ivy	
Coriaria	Golden pothos	
Cornflower	Hellebore	
Cornstalk plant	Henbane	

Nephytis	Pothos	Sweet pea
Oleander	Primrose	Swiss cheese plant
Onion	Privet	Tansy mustard
Oriental lily	Rhododendron	Tiger lily
Peace lily	Ribbon plant	Tobacco
Peony	Rosemary pea	Tomato plant
Periwinkle	Rubber plant	Tulip
Philodendron	Sago palm	Wisteria
Poinciana	Schefflera	Yews
Poinsettia	Snowdrops	
Poppy	String of pearls	

Other household dangers include mothballs, potpourri oils, essential oils, dishwashing detergents, corroded batteries, and dryer fabric softener sheets. In addition to ingesting those items, your cat could potentially suffer from ingesting tinsel from holiday trees, tiny pieces of broken toys, and small pieces of string that she likes to play with. Finally, many cat parents have heard about the dangers of window blind cords choking children. That same danger is also a potential for your cat. Toms and tabbies love to play with the dangling cords, possibly pretending they are extra long tails of rats, but if those cords end in a loop, the cats can potentially choke themselves.

Animal Poison Control Center's Top 10 pet poisons of 2009

The following is the top ten toxins that most frequently caused pet owners to call the Animal Poison Control Center of the ASPCA:

1. Human medications
2. Insecticides
3. People food
4. Plants
5. Veterinary medications (overdosing)
6. Rodenticides (rat and mouse poisons, mole and vole killers)
7. Household cleaners
8. Heavy metals (lead, zinc, mercury exposures)
9. Garden products (fertilizers, weed control)
10. Chemical hazards (antifreeze, paint thinner, drain cleaner, pool cleaner)

One final note about potential dangers in the house: Uncooked bread or pizza dough can be dangerous. Yeast is not technically a toxin, but can cause great harm in your cat if he or she should be tempted to sample some dough left in a warm spot to rise. Unbaked yeast dough can continue rising in the stomach of your cat and cause gas to build up. There is a report about a dog that ate raw dough and was taken to the veterinarian when the owner realized he was in pain. The vet was forced to surgically open the abdomen of the dog or else risk the stomach or intestines rupturing. Though obviously dangerous to dogs, rising dough may not be an issue for cats. According to Dusty Rainbolt of the Cat Writers Association, cats are probably too smart to eat it. At any rate, it is better to be safe than sorry. Keep your cat out of the kitchen if you are baking bread.

Pet Emergency: Whom Do You Call?

Perhaps while discussing the potential for toxic exposures, a note should be made about having emergency contact information at the ready. Many people have a list on the refrigerator for whom the baby sitter should call in case of emergency. Cat owners should have a similar list posted detailing the names and numbers of professionals to call in case there is an emergency of the feline persuasion. That list should include:

1. **The veterinarian:** Your cat's vet should be available to you in case of an emergency or if you have a question that you cannot answer without his or her guidance.

2. **Emergency veterinary clinic in the area:** Many pet parents do not know the services available to them other than their vet's name and number, but what if your vet is unavailable? Use the Veterinary Emergency and Critical Care Society (VECCS) website (**www.veccs. org/hospital_directory.php**) to locate an emergency clinic near you.

3. **The ASPCA's Animal Poison Control Center:** This service is available 24 hours a day and 365 days a year. To contact a trained veterinary toxicologist call 1-888-426-4435. *(Please note that a service fee of $65 will be applied to your credit card for using this service.)*

Similarly, helpful websites to keep bookmarked on your computer include, the ASPCA's Animal Poison Control information (**www.aspca.org/pet-care/ poison-control**), and Cat Advisors Online (**www.cat-advisors-online.com**).

If you believe your cat has eaten something potentially poisonous, if it is not a life-or-death emergency situation, find as much "evidence" as you can — candy wrapper, half-eaten fruit, or anything else potentially suspect, so that you can be explicit when explaining to a veterinarian or other professional exactly what and about how much you believe the cat ate. Of course, if your cat is unconscious, vomiting, or behaving as if in dire distress, you may not have the time to look for any clues. If this is the case, call your veterinarian immediately.

As you can see, your cat has unique nutritional and dietary requirements that can easily be met with a good diet and the use of supplements when needed. Commercial pet foods promise to make it easy for a cat owner to fulfill those requirements with conveniently packaged kibble and wet foods. On the surface, it may seem as if sticking with those manufactured foods would be the easiest and most cost-effective methods of giving your cat the nutrition and energy source he or she needs, but a closer look may suggest the opposite. The next chapter will address the history and role of commercially prepared cat foods.

CHAPTER
2

Trends in Commercial Pet Food

. . . .

The pet food industry started in the 1930s, and like all industries, it has changed and evolved in response to market demands, product research and development, and even commercial trends. In their ongoing attempts to stay in business, pet food manufacturers are constantly striving to provide what they believe cat owners want to feed their cats, while still making a decent profit. Companies that began providing canned foods — made from meat products left over after animals were butchered for human consumption — are now offering a variety of products made from chicken and other animals and incorporating grains and vegetables. Today, there are literally hundreds of commercially prepared foods and treats available on store shelves, from Internet-based suppliers, and from veterinarian offices. Each product boasts a label that suggests it is the best one for all cats, but it can be quite the daunting task for a caring cat owner to find out what is really inside those cans and bags of food. Even when products claim specific health and nutritional benefits, the truth of the matter is, only cat owners who buy the ingredients and prepare their cat's food themselves know what is really going into their pet's food dish.

History of the Pet Food Industry

Though humans and cats have cohabitated for thousands of years, cat owners have only been feeding their pets' commercial food for about 100 years. James Spratt, an American electrician living in London who made dog biscuits out of wheat, vegetables, and meat, created the first foods produced. His idea for prepackaged dog treats caught on, and soon pet food manufacturers were creating and marketing special treats for dogs and cats in Europe and the United States. The treats were made from a mixture of the leftover grains and vegetables that were deemed unfit for human consumption. Often the food was moldy, mildewed, or otherwise spoiled. It seemed the "special" treats were not that special.

Unaware of the true ingredients in the products, pet owners enjoyed and even began to rely on the convenience of purchasing the treats. And soon, after World War I, the Ken-L-Ration brand of dog food appeared, selling canned whole meals as dog food. The initial products consisted primarily of horsemeat, because it was a convenient way to dispose of the thousands of horses who died during the war. Eventually, in the 1930s, Gaines Food Company introduced canned cat food that contained, in addition to horse, cow, pig, and poultry, parts that remained after those animals were butchered for human consumption. Almost immediately, other companies followed Gaines's lead and started producing their own foods and treats. In fact, for companies such as Nabisco and General Mills pet foods became a way to make use of the meat by-products that were left over after preparing canned goods for humans. They were able to increase their profits, because they now had more offerings to sell, while reducing the amount of waste they created. The concept caught on, and by the 1950s, pet food became a $200 million dollar industry.

During the 1980s, the Baby Boom generation realized they were now aging, over-30 adults, and, as they do so well, they rebelled. Only this time their rebellion was not against the government, the capitalist system, or any other authoritative figures. This time they rebelled against themselves. They took aim at their new adversaries — protruding waistlines, sagging cheeks, and flapping underarms. From that, a new fad began — the fitness craze. Never before had humans focused to such an intense degree on their physical health and the various ways to maintain it. People began exercising and making wiser food choices, and because they realized their diet played a huge role in their overall health, they sought to change it for the better. One of the most popular changes made was to rely more on fresh, whole foods to replace the processed, prepackaged ones they had been stuffing themselves with. They realized fresh food not only tasted better, but also the nutrition available in it was often higher than processed foods, and it contained fewer calories. Whole, natural foods became a win-win opportunity for them. They were able to enjoy better tasting foods that were also healthier.

As health awareness grew from a trend and into a movement, perhaps it is only natural that people started looking closer at their pets' food to see what they were giving their animal companions. What pet owners discovered was that many pet food manufacturers acted like typical companies — they tried to maximize their profits by using the cheapest ingredients they could find and then sell their products at the highest margin their customers would pay. The results were cat foods and treats made with products most owners' did not feel comfortable feeding to their beloved pets.

Unfortunately, there are few laws that prevent rancid, moldy foods and other unsavory items from being put into our pets' food. The leftover products that humans cannot eat continue to be used to make pet food today. And though cats do eat the whole animal in the wild, they rarely eat the whole exterior of the animal. Things like claws, beaks, chicken feet, hooves, and teeth that wild cats would leave behind, can be ground up, labeled "meat by-products," and put in cans and bags by pet food manufacturers.

As health-conscious pet owners learned what they were feeding their cats, they began to demand better products from the pet food industry. In reply, premium brands emerged offering foods with what promised to be more wholesome ingredients. Pet product manufacturers also began offering foods aimed toward animals in various stages of their lives, from kitten to nursing mother to senior cat. Then, the industry realized they had a market for formulas specially designed for cats with particular health needs, such as diabetes and chronic renal failure.

Today, pet owners have a variety of products, food, and treats to offer their cats. The whole gamut of quality materials can be found at just about any price, and pet owners continue to buy whatever they can for their pets. Though the industry may be changing, Americans remain steadfast in their commitment to their pets. According to the American Pet Products Association, more households in the United States have pets than they have children. Those pet owners spend more money on pet food than on baby food, and the pet food industry is proving to be recession-proof. By 2007, it was a $15 billion industry.

Continuing Problems with the Pet Food Industry

Pet food manufacturers are trying to improve the quality of their products, but the fact remains that the vast majority of what is available on market shelves is of poor quality. Even the better products sold in specialty pet stores contain fillers, such as wheat gluten and corn meal that cats cannot tolerate, and chemicals you would neither feed yourself, nor your cats. Pet owners continue to be disappointed by the contents listed on the packages, and there remains little governmental oversight aimed at preventing dangerous products and unhealthy fillers from being used as pet food ingredients.

It is an unfortunate fact that fillers in pet foods are often corn- and wheat-based. Cats do not digest those carbohydrates very well at all. It may seem like your tabby is doing fine right now on a bag of corn-laced kibble, but he or she may not do well on it long-term. Because of the difficulty in digesting those carbohydrates, your cat may become overweight by eating them on a regular basis over the course of his or her lifetime. In fact, many veterinarians believe chronic health problems, such as feline diabetes and irritable bowel syndrome, can be tied to eating commercial foods with corn and/or wheat in them over the lifetime of a cat.

Fillers are not the only worry when it comes to what is in your pet's food. There are no requirements that pet food products have pre-market approval by the FDA or any other regulating agency. There are only standards concerning how ingredients are listed and the nutrient density of the products companies should follow that are set by the Association of American Feed Control Officials (AAFCO), the Food and Drug Administration's Center for Veterinarian Medicine (FDA/CVM), and the Pet Food Institute (PFI).

In general, the AAFCO requires all foods labeled "complete and balanced" to meet what they consider to be the nutritional needs of a cat as listed in their annual report on dog and cat food nutrient profiles. However, that organization does not mandate that all cat food be complete and balanced. They do not pass judgment on whether or not an ingredient is good for your cat, although they do provide definitions of terms used to label ingredients. To do that, the AAFCO puts out a publication every year called the Official Publication that addresses how labels of pet food products can be worded. It just does not specify the kind of ingredients that can be placed inside the containers. For example, when a pet food label says "animal protein" is in the product, it can mean anything from the healthy meat of a cow to a cancerous tumor or other diseased tissues from any animal, road kill, leftover meat from slaughterhouses, and even "rendered animals" (stray dogs and cats that were sheltered and euthanized). In fact, in 1990, the *San Francisco Chronicle* detailed how millions of dead dogs and cats wound up in pet food. The Canadian Veterinary Medical Association, the American Veterinary Medical Association, and the U.S. Food and Drug Administration confirmed the findings even though pet food manufacturers tried to deny it.

Those same regulations say the definition of "meat" can be used to mean cows, pigs, goats, sheep, or other animals. "Meat by-products" can include heads, feet, bones, intestines, lungs, spleens, and more. The term "meat-and-bone-meal" means that the materials put in the product were not used fresh, but were rendered. "Render" is an industrial term that specifies the way carcasses are handled. To render an animal, after butchering the remaining carcass is dropped into a giant vat of boiling water and cooked for several hours to separate the fat. After the article in the *San Francisco Chronicle* appeared, the FDA studied commercial pet food to look for a chemical called pentobarbital. It is used to euthanize stray animals at pounds and shelters. And yes, they found it. Products listing "meat-and-bone-meal" were the ones most likely to be found to contain pentobarbital. Unfortunately, even though the *Chronicle* article drew quite a bit of attention to the belief that euthanized animals were used in pet food, and the Veterinary Medical Associations confirmed the findings, nothing really changed. Pet food manufacturers continue to insist they do not use such ingredients and never have, but there are no laws against these actions, so there is no legal body directly overseeing the issue.

Aside from the quality and origin of the ingredients in our pet's food, pet owners also are becoming increasingly concerned about the safety of those ingredients as well. Every year, there are several pet food and treat recalls due to spoiled or tainted ingredients. Perhaps the biggest scare was 2007's massive recall when, after hundreds of pets suffered and died from them, 150 different brands of food comprising more than 5,000 separate pet food products were recalled, meaning the products had to be removed from store shelves and destroyed so they could not be sold to consumers. The FDA and USDA investigation found the food to be intentionally contaminated with the chemical melamine. Melamine is a plasticide, but when put in food products, it can make the food appear to contain a higher percentage of protein than it really does. The contaminated foods were recalled and the Chinese and American corporate officials of the companies involved in the incident were indicted by a federal grand jury, but pet food recalls continue. In fact, pet food recalls are not rare at all. The 2007 recall stands out and is well known because of the sheer size, scope, and number of animals affected. But pet food recalls occur on a regular basis. They happen so frequently that the American Humane Society keeps a running list of all recalls and investigations of potential pet food and treat problems on its website: **www. humanesociety.org**. According to the site, there were more than 20 recalls in 2009, and the months of January, March, and April 2010 each saw different pet food recalls and investigations, every one of which involved potential salmonella, a common culprit of food poisonings. Also, in March of that year, the FDA began an investigation of Dynamic Pet Products after receiving reports of dogs becoming ill and even dying after eating their treats. That makes four recalls in as many months, suggesting that commercial pet foods can still be risky.

Veterinarians on Cat Nutrition

As pet owners become increasingly disenchanted with commercial pet food, they find their only other option is to provide natural foods for their pets. Pet owners are finding support from some, but not all, veterinarians who are equally disturbed and distrusting of the pet food industry. Many veterinarians are noticing that on average, the domestic cat's life expectancy is increasing, but the numbers of food-related disease is also increasing, as are cancers, kidney diseases, hyperthyroidism, and autoimmune disorders that could potentially be linked to poor diets.

Unfortunately, not all veterinarians are on the same page. Most veterinarians receive very little diet and nutrition instruction during their tenure at college. That small amount of instruction is generally done under the auspices of large, commercial pet food manufacturers, who either donated to the school or who set up large research facilities there. It is very hard to believe that a bias toward commercial cat food does not exist. As Robin Olson, Cat Writer's Association member and multi-cat owner, found out, it also means that you may have to put up a fight with your veterinarian.

When Olson's cat was diagnosed with diabetes, the veterinarian explained to her that it was necessary to feed the cat a dry kibble and canned food that was primarily made of grain. She balked at the idea. He persisted and began offering her pamphlets and literature that he received from the pet food manufacturer.

The information explained the food was created in a sterile environment and safety-tested on cats. Olson still felt uncomfortable with the idea and continued to refuse his advice. Instead, she opted to put her cat on a grain-free, raw diet. Within four weeks, her cat's diagnosis was changed — he was no longer diabetic and was taken completely off insulin.

Olson now takes her cat to a homeopathic veterinarian who supports feeding a raw, grain-free diet to her cats. A homeopathic veterinarian is a holistic, or integrative, animal doctor who takes into consideration all facets of a cat's life. A traditional veterinarian will diagnose a disease or disorder and then prescribe treatment for that particular health issue. A holistic veterinarian, on the other hand, will diagnose a disease or disorder, prescribe treatment for it, but will also look at the diet, behavior, and environment of the animal to see if there are ways of altering any of them to make the cat's overall health improve. Your cat's holistic vet might want to know more about your cat than you ever thought about. He or she may ask questions regarding your cat's family history as well as complete medical history. The vet will want to know all about your cat's sleep and play patterns, whether or not he or she is housebound or spends much time outside, if he or she shares the human family with other animals, and how many humans there are in the household and their ages. *For more of Olson's story, see Chapter 4.*

Your cat's diet will be of primary interest to a holistic veterinarian. According to holistic philosophy, proper nutrition is at the core of repairing and healing all health and wellness issues your cat may ever face. Holistic vets believe your cat's body has a beautiful system to repair and heal itself, and that that system runs on nutrition. The vitamins, minerals, and phytonutrients that are naturally present in fresh, whole foods are tailor-made to replenish and refuel cells so they can rebuild tissue and fight off disease. Because the processing of food to become commercial kibble or canned products depletes the natural nutrient density of the original foods, most holistic veterinarians believe you should be feeding your cats fresh, whole foods, so they get the nutrition in its purest form.

Holistic treatment modalities generally affect the cats' lifestyle, but in a positive, appropriate, and minimally invasive way. Holistic veterinarians understand cats can become stressed, and changes will compound the stress, so they strive to make all treatments as easy on the cat as possible. They work equally hard not to allow a treatment for one disease or disorder to create another issue. Side effects are not accepted as a necessary evil in the holistic point of view.

If you find your traditional veterinarian is not in support of you making changes to your cat's diet, try finding a holistic or homeopathic one. You can search the database of the American Holistic Veterinary Medical Association's referral search website, **www.holisticvetlist.com.** Otherwise, you may need to be prepared to educate your cat's veterinarian the next time you walk into his or her office. Be prepared, be sure you thoroughly research the nutritional needs of your cat, and have a complete understanding of how diet impacts his or her health.

Holistic? Homeopathic? How are they different?

Holistic veterinarians focus on the health of the whole animal and take into consideration its diet, environment, and lifestyle to determine a path and regimen that will lead the animal to optimum levels of good health.

Homeopathic veterinarians are holistic in their approach, but they are also schooled in homeopathic remedies, which are natural products that encourage the body's own immune response to heal itself.

The commercial pet food industry is not an evil and insidious entity. In fact, although the current methods of producing foods may seem a bit lacking when it comes to quality and purity, attempts are being made to increase the number of natural and organic pet foods in the market. More and more companies are looking to improve the nutritional quality of cat foods while continuing to provide the convenience of prepackaged meals. Perhaps one day, cat owners will be able to walk the aisles of available pet foods and only find meals and treats that are of high-quality meats and vegetables, tailored to their cat's unique nutritional requirements.

CHAPTER
3

The Natural Pet Food Industry

. . . .

As pet owners continue to become discouraged and disappointed with commercial pet foods and the lack of government oversight regarding the safety of those foods, they are turning to natural products for their feeding options with the belief that they are safer and healthier than commercial, prepackaged foods. Though the numbers of those owners grow, so do the reports of cats benefiting from being taken off commercial foods and placed on a natural diet. In direct response to the new demand for natural foods, pet food manufacturers are trying to provide more wholesome, higher-quality foods than they have ever produced before. Some pet owners and veterinarians are even entering the industry by creating their own line of natural foods to help other cat owners join what they see as a movement. Now, cat owners have several options for finding natural foods — even treats — for their purring kitties.

Who's on the Natural Bandwagon & Why?

The demographics detailing the number of owners feeding their cats natural foods is difficult to pinpoint exactly, because there are no national organizations for people to join or from which to conduct surveys. However, sales statistics gathered by the American Pet Products Association (APPA), may reveal a trend away from commercial foods.

According to the APPA, total expenditures on commercial products for pets in 2008 were $45.5 billion, and the projected sales for 2010 are $47.7 billion, a 4.83 percent increase. Food-only purchases totaled $17.56 billion in 2008 and are projected to be $18.28 billion in 2010, which, at a 4.1 percent increase, suggests slightly slower growth than total sales. Meanwhile, miscellaneous supplies and over-the-counter medicines (grouped together by the APPA) and veterinary care are both expected to climb by 5.7 percent, a rate higher than total sales. So, while it appears that pet owners are still more than willing to buy products for their pets, they are not buying commercial food with the same enthusiasm, as they are other items. And their medical expenses seem to be taking more and more of their dollar.

A quick Internet search will pull up literally thousands of cat owners with stories to tell about why they made the switch from commercial feed to home-based, natural foods. They come from all walks of life, all ethnicities, and from cities to rural areas. All are united in their quest to give their cats what they feel to be the best foods possible.

CASE STUDY:
A COMMON SENSE APPROACH
TO FEEDING YOUR CAT

John Wood, co-founder
U.S. Wellness Meats
PO Box 9
Monticello, Missouri 63457

The goal of U.S. Wellness Meats is to provide animal protein sources of the purest foods possible. In fact, their slogan is "Our animals eat right so you can too!" Originally, their meat products were intended for human consumption, but as co-founder John Wood reports, in 2003 they realized their largest grass-fed liver customer was actually buying the meat for cats — 75 cats that the customer catered to in a specially constructed mansion near Naples, Florida. U.S. Wellness Meats then realized that pet owners went to extraordinary measures to provide the very best nutrition for their pets. So, Wood and his company broadened their customer base by supplying pet owners with their food products.

As the company started catering to pet owners, they started researching the health benefits of natural food products and found extremely motivating evidence in studies by Price Pottenger.

One study involved nearly 900 cats and covered three generations over a period of ten years.

The study broke the cats into three groups: One was fed a diet of a raw meat, and a mixture of raw milk and cod-liver oil; the second group was given a diet that was cooked meat and raw milk and cod-liver oil; the last group was fed an all-raw meat diet. It was only the last group, the one eating only raw meat, that thrived and remained healthy throughout all three generations. At the time of the study, however, taurine's impact on a cat's health was unknown, so the cats that received the cooked food in the study did not receive adequate amounts of taurine.

Even though there are so many pet owners whose cats achieve optimum levels of good health on natural foods, it is still difficult to spread the word to cat owners who continue to rely on commercially prepared foods. Woods believes that is because of the mountain of advertising touted by the prepared pet food makers who can afford to spend millions of dollars convincing pet owners their prepared cooked pet food message is steeped in science. Woods believes if all pet owners would use a common sense approach when feeding their pets and think about how a pet's ancestors used to live, they would feed them all-natural raw foods. And he asks, when was the last time you saw a lion waiting to be spoon-fed out of a can of synthetic cat food?

Benefits Owners Have Witnessed from Natural Pet Food

Pet owners who have made the switch from commercial to natural pet foods seem to have the same result — healthier, happier pets. The most frequent benefit mentioned is one of weight loss on obese cats. It appears that cats on "diet" commercial cat food do not lose as much weight as cats on a natural diet, probably because of the grain products used as low-calorie fillers in many of the prepackaged foods. Coinciding with the weight loss, many owners like Robin Olson, whose experience with an unsupportive veterinarian was mentioned earlier, even claim they were able to put an end to their cat's suffering from diabetes.

Supporting the holistic veterinary theory that proper nutrition allows the body to heal are various reports that symptoms from serious autoimmune diseases, such as rheumatoid arthritis, decreased with a natural foods diet. Additionally, the various gastrointestinal and urinary tract health issues cats frequently suffer all seem to abate, and even disappear once a cat is completely on natural food. For example, cats with cancer seem to have more energy; cats post-surgery often heal faster, and senior cats seem to have a longer, higher-quality lifespan.

Other cat owners report benefits including, the clearing up of skin and hair issues, healthier ears and eyes, and fewer allergic reactions. Many even believe a natural diet is a turnoff to pests such as fleas and parasites. They say that their cats no longer get fleas or only get a few, compared to what they suffered with when eating prepackaged food. Still others claim their cats are happier than they were when they were being fed a commercial diet. In fact, it is very difficult to find a cat owner who feels feeding his or her cat an all-natural diet is a detriment to the animal.

CASE STUDY: CHOOSING A NATURAL DIET

Sally E. Bahner
Member, Cat Writers'
Association
sebahner@snet.net

The following is an excerpt from a Case Study with Sally E. Bahner. She has more than 30 years of experience as a writer and editor, spending the last 15 years specializing in cat-related issues. Her primary focus is cat nutrition, holistic care, and multiple cat behaviors. She recently started offering services as a feline behavior and care consultant. Bahner is member of the Cat Writers' Association from which she has received the Muse Medallion in 1999, 2000, 2001, 2008, and 2009, as well as several Certificates of Excellence. She resides in Branford, Connecticut, with her husband, Paul, and their four cats: Dusty, Pulitzer, Mollie, and a Russian Blue named Tekla, who came after Sara, her other Russian Blue.

Bahner was always interested in improving her cats' diet. As editor of *The Whole Cat Journal*, she had the opportunity to read about and explore all aspects of cat nutrition, diet, and foods.

She first looked into the premade raw diets. There were only a few companies who offered food supplies at the time, roughly 10 years ago. Eventually she created her own recipe, based on the knowledge she continued to acquire so she could custom-tailor the diet for her cats. It was also less expensive because she had multiple cats.

It was not long before she learned firsthand the power of raw foods. Her Russian Blue, Sara, developed mammary cancer. Through her research, she learned that the carbohydrates and sugars in commercial foods could feed the cancer. Bahner doubled her efforts to make raw food for Sara, who wound up doing well for much longer than most cats with mammary cancer.

As she continued learning more about cat nutrition, Bahner began reading labels of commercially prepared cat food.

In her opinion, given the definitions of various ingredients and the way their meanings could be manipulated, the manufacturers could make shoe soles sound like a viable diet. Also, the foods were filled with carbohydrates — which cats do not require — yet dry foods are loaded with them because they are needed for part of the extrusion process, where nutrients are sprayed onto food.

The biggest hurdle she has had to face when it comes to convincing pet owners that raw foods are best for their cats is the marketing by major pet food companies. The message that commercial foods are superior to anything else you could feed your cats is so ingrained into the psyche of pet owners that they are afraid to experiment. It can sometimes be difficult to convince them even to feed a variety of commercial brands. Look at the images on TV; veterinarians who usually discourage feeding raw food are backing the commercial companies because their nutritional information comes from the likes of Hill's or other pet food manufacturers.

The salmonella/bacteria scare tactics are employed, but because cats have a short intestinal tract, such bacterial issues seldom affect them. As for humans, it is a matter of good housekeeping: Wash your hands, dishes, and utensils in hot, soapy water.

People often say they do not have time to prepare their cat's food, or they are afraid of not doing it correctly, but a lot of information is available to guide them. Once you find a recipe that works for you and your cats, it is not difficult. Although many people grind up whole birds or toss out mice, you do not have to go that far. It is okay to supplement with an occasional can of good quality commercial food.

Cats have to be transitioned into a raw diet. Because real food is not full of the flavorings that are added by commercial pet food manufacturers to increase appeal of their foods, cats may not immediately be attracted to it; this is why some people may give up too quickly. Bahner believes you can sprinkle some freeze-dried chicken treats, dried bonito flakes, ground-up dry food on top, or add a smear of canned food to give it more flavor. It does take some time and patience because the likes of kibble is so addicting. Always remember, you are the boss. We equate food with love for our cats, and if they love the food, they love us. Just keep repeating the mantra — cats are carnivores, they need meat.

Traditional Companies Making the Switch to Natural

Pet food manufacturers have not been blind to the shrinking sales margin of their food products in recent years. To make up for those slowing numbers, they have been busily introducing new "natural" and "organic" products for pets. In fact, as reported on **www.packagedfacts.com**, such product sales increased by nearly $527 million in 2004, and topped $1 billion in 2009. Clearly, the trend toward natural pet products is steadily growing.

Traditional pet food manufacturers are now offering natural and organic foods in addition to their lower quality, cheaper products. But, though the ingredients are indeed more pure and natural, they continue to use highly automated manufacturing technologies to produce them. The products remain processed kibble and canned food, neither one of which resembles the original meat products that are supposed to be in the ingredients, and both are filled with preservatives.

Processing commercial cat foods — dry kibble, moist kibble, and canned — calls for extreme measures regardless of how natural the products start out. Kibble, in particular, undergoes a process that first strips all nutrition out of the food before artificially replacing it. To create kibble, manufacturers must dehydrate, pulp, and grind the whole food ingredients, after which those ingredients are mixed and pressed into little pellets to form its kibble shape. Next, comes a process called extrusion, where the kibble is placed under high heat and pressure while synthetic vitamins and minerals are sprayed onto it to make up for whatever nutrition was lost during the initial processing of the original ingredients. Fat with preservatives in it is often sprayed over top of the food to make it more palatable to your cat. There is nothing in nature equivalent to extrusion; it is simply not a natural process.

Actually, it is very difficult to pinpoint what natural really means when it comes to pet products. It is a loose term that companies can pretty much define for themselves as they create their products. When used to label human foods, natural means there are no synthetically made ingredients in the products. That definition pretty much holds true for pet food, but most companies put their own twist on it as well. Some pet food producers of natural products use the word to signify they use foods and treats that are pesticide- and toxin-free. For others, natural means there are no added colorings or flavorings in the products. There are pet food producers who boast their foods contain natural ingredients because they only use protein products that have received the United States Department of Agriculture's stamp of approval. And yet others say "natural" for them means the chicken meat came from free-range, cage-free fowl, none of their meats were injected with hormones or antibiotics, and all the products were sustainably farmed. The most expensive pet foods labeled "natural" are those that include all of the above in their definition of the word.

Pet owners creating natural start-ups

Fed up with the inability to know exactly what was in a natural product, new upstart companies came on to the pet food scene to try and create healthier pet foods. Cat owners who successfully cured or halted the progression of disease in their own pets through diet and wanted to share what made their cats healthy with other pet owners started many of these companies, for example Wild Kitty (**www.wildkitty.com**). Others, such as the Honest Kitchen (**www. honestkitchen.com**), just wanted to provide their pets with what they thought was the best food they could create as a proactive step to keep their kitties healthy for as long as possible.

Alongside the pet owners developing their own companies are the organizations that entered the natural pet market, intent on providing a better quality of foods for all pets. Those companies often develop products under the advice and guidance of veterinarians. One such company is Life's Abundance All-Natural Pet Food (**www.healthypetslife.com**), which is formulated by Dr. Jane Bicks. Bicks and other veterinarians on a mission to reverse the increase of cancers, autoimmune disorders, and other health conditions they are seeing in their animal patients. These newer companies tend to ignore putting the emphasis on the most cost-effective forms of manufacturing their food products. Instead, they are opting to provide your pets food that looks, feels, smells, and tastes as if it were wild prey, even if it means higher operating costs and lower profit margins.

What do natural companies make for cats?

Natural pet food companies make the same kind of products for cats that commercial companies do, only they do it more naturally. They avoid fillers and unwholesome by-products to provide muscle and organ meat directly from chickens, ducks, fish, and turkeys. Some even have clams and the tropical seafood specialty — conch — available for a kitty with a Caribbean palate. Other companies promise pure ingredients, with little tampering from men and machines. The primary goal for all these businesses is simply to create products that mimic nature's original food for cats. Most started out offering frozen foods, but now, even a kibble-type of dry food, moist mixtures, and treats can be purchased from the natural companies. And a new service is offered to pet owners as well: Wild Kitty has created "make-your-own" kits where you can personally choose the ingredients based on your tabby's particular likes and dislikes. Those companies will package your order according to what you choose and deliver it to you overnight, packed in ice.

Once they established themselves with repeat customers, many of the natural companies branched out into other areas of cat and pet products. The Honest Kitchen and other companies now offer natural, animal- and plant-based nutritional supplements that do not contain food coloring, artificial flavors, or any other additives. They are even creating pet treats aimed at helping particular health issues. For example, Healthy Pet Net offers treats with extra omega-3 fatty acids for healthier skin and hair, and other companies are working on adding glucosamine to treats for pets with arthritis or other joint problems.

Along with food and treats, natural companies are expanding even further to offer non-edible, non-food-related pet products. Bedding made from organic materials and fabrics that do not emit off gassing or formaldehyde are now available for your cat to rest upon, and toys from recycled products and filled with organic stuffing are available for kittens. Grooming items, travel accessories, litter boxes, and other plastic or wood-based items for your cats can be found with labels boasting their non-toxic and natural nature. There are also a variety of options for natural litter and even odor and stain removers created from natural, plant based enzymes. Demand for such products has grown to the point where you can now purchase many of these products in your large chain pet stores, such as PetSmart, as well as in small, sole proprietorship stores, such as the Wagging Tail Pet Nutrition Center in Cape May, New Jersey. Whole Foods Markets and other natural health food stores for people are now also carrying natural pet products and even some raw foods for your cats.

Many of these companies are animal specific, meaning they cater only to cats, or dogs, or to a particular farm animal. Though as they find profitable success with their target animals, some corporations do expand to offer supplies to other species or even to the big cats and other carnivores at zoos.

How natural can you get?

Apparently, the length owners will go to give their cats the best, most natural life has no bounds. On June 16, 2010, The New York Times reported on a growing trend among cat owners: extending their homes by building "catios."

What is a catio? It is an enclosed outdoor space where an otherwise indoor cat can go to get fresh air, watch the birds and butterflies, and yet remain safely guarded from the Rottweiler next door. In other words, it is a place where cats have a safe opportunity to spend time in the natural, great outdoors. In the big cities, catios are appearing on apartment balconies, condominium rooftops, and even on some fire-escape stairwells. However, if you take a quick drive to the less urban areas, you fill find catios can be quite extravagant protective bubbles, complete with tunnels, playgrounds, and scratching posts for suburbanite felines.

Most catios are of the do-it-yourself variety, limited only by the cat owner's skill and budget. They are made with two-by-four boards, chicken wire, PVC pipes, and whatever else the cat owner can find at a building supply store that will work. Now there are ready-made enclosures on the market. Kittywalk Systems sells modular enclosures made of tubes and rooms that can be custom-designed for every cat style (check them out at **www.kittywalksystems.com**).

How long have natural cat foods been produced?

Because humans have kept cats as pets for thousands of years prior to the industrial revolution, a case could be made saying that they have always provided natural cat food. However, the same cannot be said for corporate entities. Many see Sojourner Farms as the first commercial, natural pet food manufacturer. They came on the scene in the mid-1980s with the idea of creating simple, back-to-basics, "real" food for pets.

For some reason, the first natural pet food companies were focused on dog food — probably because cat owners know how their felines generally do not like change, and they wanted to be sure it was a good idea. So why not let the dogs be guinea pigs? The emphasis was originally on food only — complete meals for your pets either in kibble form or a moist product served from sealed packets. As the movement caught on, more companies started forming, and more food products were created, such as treats and supplements. With each addition, the goal remained to use only natural, whole-food ingredients from sustainable farms.

What goes into testing, research, and development?

Because there still remains a lack of government oversight on pet food manufacturers, there are no guidelines regarding product testing or research. Each company has its own policies and self-regulates according to what it feels is important quality standards. However, there is very little transparency. As with all industries, it is important for manufacturers to try and keep company recipes and techniques out of public eye. Otherwise, they risk being copied by competitors and put out of business. Pet owners must go on faith that when the labels say "pure beef" that, indeed, there is real beef inside.

Each company has its own protocol for testing, research, and development. Because the majority of natural pet food manufacturers started with one person looking to create a better life for his or her personal pet, most of those companies have their roots in trial and error. There is no real testing in the sense of using clinical trials to determine the health benefits of particular foods, but there is often real-life testing that provides anecdotal evidence. Someone's tabby did well with a high protein, chicken-based diet, and someone else's tom faired equally on it, so the company is producing foods that reflect that diet.

The majority of research for each company seems to be based on looking at a cat's diet in the wild, comparing it to what our domestic cat's wild ancestors ate, and coming up with an approximate ideal food. Development is ongoing as new discoveries continue to be made regarding the nutritional makeup of those foods, which companies then must try to mimic for our modern felines. As veterinarians — and owners — continue to find correlations between foods and health issues, more experimenting is completed via trial and error with their own cats. Few, if any, natural pet food companies have the financial resources of a Purina or Hill's to conduct clinical, scientific research, which could be a good thing. If they must research with their own pets, whom they love and adore, you can usually assume they are only looking for what is for the highest good of the animal — not what would be the cheapest way to supply vitamin A to it.

Natural product marketing and market share

Natural pet food companies could not exist without the Internet. Though they do have some shelf space in local pet supply stores, their products are not found in supermarkets. The fresh nature of their foods requires frequent turnover of stock, otherwise they risk losing the ingredients to rotting, fermenting, and mold growth. That means that pet store companies must be convinced the products will sell, and sell quickly, lest they risk losing money on inventory that is taking up space that could be filled with foods that will not spoil or rot so quickly. It is just like when humans shop for high-quality steak: They cannot find it in a box at the local discount department store. There is an expiration date on the foods, requiring them to be sold relatively quickly.

For the most part, natural food companies must rely on pet owners searching them out, learning about them via word of mouth, or recommendations from veterinarians. They also advertise by affiliate marketing on pet-related websites and educational blogs, and they get as much airtime as they can on radio and television programs. The good news is that because the demand continues to increase, brick-and-mortar stores are now popping up dedicated to offering natural pet products. One of the largest is Only Natural Pet Store. It was originally an Internet-only based company offering the entire gamut of pet-related natural products: foods, treats, supplements, bedding, toys, grooming items, collars, leashes, and holistic care products. Because business grew to such an extreme, Only Natural Pet Store opened its first brick-and-mortar facility in Boulder, Colorado, and the company is expecting to grow and open more.

A new trend on the horizon

No longer content in trying to improve our own physical health via returning to more natural foods, humans are now looking to improve the global health of our world by living more natural lifestyles. And the Only Natural Pet Store could very well be emblematic of this trend that seems to be replacing the fitness trend of the 1980s. The company philosophy is based on what is best for the earth. Their building is powered completely by wind energy. Their packaging materials are reused and recycled boxes and biodegradable packing peanuts to have the smallest impact on the environment. All of their paper is 100-percent recycled. They try their best to partner up with manufacturers who share their values. And they even encourage their employees to lower their own carbon footprint by biking to work or using public transportation. They are a very natural company, indeed.

CASE STUDY: BENEFITS OF A RAW DIET

Deb Teubert
Animal Holistic Health
Practitioner 960-622-5532
www.debteuvert.com

Deb Teubert is an animal holistic health practitioner in Wisconsin, who is a strong advocate for feeding our pets natural foods. She often prescribes a raw foods diet for cats to prevent and even cure a variety of health issues.

Teubert's Siamese cat, Simi, whom she loved dearly, was the catalyst of change for her. Simi was diagnosed with pancreatitis. She was in severe pain and the veterinary community could only offer Teubert the option of euthanasia to relieve her pain. Teubert refused to believe that was the only option for her cat. Instead, she began researching other alternatives, which included traditional Chinese medicine, raw diet, homeopathic, and supplements. As a result, Simi lived several more years on a raw diet and proper supplements.

Simi was only the beginning. Now, as an animal holistic health practitioner, Teubert sees a large number of animals with ailments caused all or in part, from commercial food: poor coat, colitis, ear infections, urinary tract inflammations, pancreatitis, skin eruptions such as hotspots, infections of the mouth and gums, arthritic pain/lameness, obesity, and gallbladder pain, to name a few. All of these ailments often disappear and do not come back when the animal's diet is changed to raw. At times, other holistic modalities, such as red light therapy, acupressure, and essential oils are also used to bring the animal back into balance, but it is the proper diet that will allow the animal to stay healthy and balanced.

Teubert admits there are two downsides to a natural or raw diet for your pet. The first is the veterinary community that still does not see the benefits of a raw diet. In fact, she says that many conventional veterinarians strongly advise against the diet, saying it puts an animal in danger of kidney problems, parasite/bacterial infections, and is bad for the cat's teeth.

The second downside is that raw food can be quite a bit more expensive than any commercially prepared food. Because of that, it is sometimes difficult to convince owners to change even though in the end, the owner will come out ahead financially because the cat will be healthier, and there will be fewer trips to the vet.

As a cat owner and as professional animal health practitioner, Teubert knows it can be challenging to change a cat to a raw diet, but she knows it can be done. A very slow gradual change in diet is needed, which may mean transitioning over several months to the new food. If only dry food has been fed to the cat, she suggests you change to a high-quality canned food and then to a raw diet. Adding a dime-sized amount of the new food to the old food for a week, then increasing by another dime-sized amount for another week, and so on is a tried and true method of transitioning. Owners who say their cat will not eat raw have tried to rush through the process too quickly. Also, poor quality cat food, dry or canned, is high in salt. Cats come to expect this flavor in their foods and often will refuse higher quality food or raw food because the salty flavor is not there. A very small pinch of sea salt added to the food mix can help ease the transition, but should be discontinued after the transition to an all-raw diet has been made. Do not add salt to a cat's diet that is in kidney failure, however.

Without question, commercially prepared natural pet foods are finding their way onto the store shelves of pet supply stores and into the homes of pet owners. However, they are not as all-encompassing as their even more widely available, less natural counterparts. Cat owners may still have difficulty finding the foods their cats want with the nutritional value they need. To that end, cats have a lot to teach their humans about how to figure it all out.

Cat Eating Habits

· ·

There are several options for feeding your cat a healthy, natural diet. You can rely on good quality commercial foods, create all the food for yourself, or do a combination of the two. But regardless of what you feed the tabby who likes to stalk you until you put the breakfast bowl down on the kitchen floor each morning, you will need to be aware that he or she has some highly specialized dining preferences and specific food needs. You should also be familiar with the foods that can harm your cat and the other toxins that may be in the environment.

Natural Menu Options for Your Cat

The menu of dining options you create for your cat can be as simple or as complex as you — and your cat — want. It is quite possible to fulfill all of your cat's nutritional requirements with just a few high-quality commercial grade food products. At the extreme opposite end of the spectrum, you can load your freezer with gourmet-quality meals you produced yourself from special-ordered meats. There are a multitude of options in between, giving you the freedom to custom tailor his or her menu to fit your lifestyle, budget, and storage space, as well as your cat's taste buds.

Feeding only high-quality commercial foods

Finding and feeding a high-quality commercial cat food might not be as easy as it sounds. You will find a variety of products on store shelves claiming to fit the bill, but you will need to take a close look at the labels and read the fine print to be sure. As mentioned earlier, the AAFCO sets the standards as to what a "complete and balanced" cat food contains as far as nutrition goes. That organization requires companies to put on the label the percentage of weight of the food that contains protein, fat, carbohydrates, and moisture. If you look at the part of a cat food label that says "Guaranteed Analysis," you will find it tells you the moisture percentage of the product as well.

What Does the Label Mean?

You will need to do a little math to determine how much protein, fat, and carbohydrates are in a container of prepackaged cat food. On the package label, the manufacturer should tell you the basic nutrition facts of the product, which is the percentage of protein, fat, and so on. There will also be a number telling you how much of the food is made from moisture. The first step to finding the protein level is to subtract the moisture percentage number from 100. That gives you the amount of dry ingredients. Next, divide that answer number into the crude protein figure on the label. The resulting number will be a close estimate of how large the portion of protein is in the food. For example, say a can of cat food has protein listed at 9 percent and moisture at 77 percent. The math would look like this:

$$100 - 77 = 23$$

$$9 \div 23 = .40 \text{ (by rounding to the nearest tenth)}$$

> Therefore the amount of protein in the product is 40 percent, which is less than the 60 to 65 percent you want to aim for in your cat's diet. You will need to repeat the process to determine how much fat is in the product by using the crude fat figure on the label as well.

Even after doing the math to determine the protein and fat ratio of the cat food, your job is not yet done. If you are determined to only feed your kitty a good, quality commercial feed, you will also need to look at the ingredient list to be sure meat by-products and poultry by-products are not in it.

There are several pet food companies trying to meet the demand for high-quality natural foods, and there are now a growing number of organic and natural packaged foods on pet store shelves. The company Natura sells several holistic pet foods under different brands, including Innova, Evo, and California Natural. Blue Buffalo is another high-quality cat food manufacturer that promises to avoid by-products and cheap fillers. However, those foods remain quite expensive. For example, a six-pound bag of Evo Dry Cat and Kitten Food from Natura can cost close to $25, and pet owners must still go on faith that the ingredients are pure and untainted.

Combining commercial with natural foods

The second option for cat parents is to supplement those high-quality, whole-food-based commercial products with homemade meals and treats. With this option, you can guarantee the safety and quality of at least part of your cat's diet while you still have the convenience of seemingly trustworthy store-bought products. If you go this route, you should choose a high-quality cat food that meets the qualifications just mentioned, with little or no grains in the ingredient list. You should definitely avoid the foods listing "meat by-products"; remember, manufacturers do not have to reveal what exactly that phrase means to them. Expect to pay a premium for those foods, as cheap pet food is very similar to cheap fast food for humans: It offers little nutrition with a bunch of calories.

This feeding option can be a tremendous help for pet owners who have cats suffering from particular health concerns, in that the food types and ratios can be tailored to meet the individual needs of your cat. For example, cats that eat commercial food and suffer from constipation can benefit from having broth poured over their foods to make the food moister, so it can move through their systems more easily. Cats with diabetes can control their blood sugar levels better on a high-protein diet, so supplementing commercial foods with quality proteins, such as organic chicken livers and meat, can help stabilize blood sugars for those cats.

When going this route with a cat that has been on an established diet of commercial food, slowly introduce the natural foods to him or her. At first, your cat may turn its nose up at anything that does not resemble canned food or dry kibble. Be sure he or she is hungry and offer the new food first, in small amounts, then follow-up with the commercial food. Be wary of the flip side — your cat may decide he or she likes the home-prepared foods better than anything out of a package. Be sure to mix the two together to help camouflage the fact that they are two different foods.

Feeding only organic and natural foods

The third option for feeding your cat is to use only natural foods you prepare yourself. The numerous benefits of going natural with your cat only begin with the issues of food safety and purity. There is also simplicity in preparing your cat's meals. You get to skip the pet food stores because you are buying your tom's food at your market. Therefore, you have one less errand to run. And while preparing food for your cat may seem like a lot of work, the process can be streamlined and incorporated into the meal preparation you do for the human members of your family. You can create relatively small batches of meals, freeze them, and keep some conveniently thawed in your refrigerator at all times. Relatively small batches would be about the size of a standard, family-of-four dinner that would feed a healthy cat two times a day for a month.

Going all natural in your cat's diet is kinder to the earth as well. You are not relying on a factory to create food that is then put into cans and bags created out of the earth's resources or out of potentially dangerous plasticides. That neglected trip to the pet food store means your car is not burning fossil fuels to go to yet one more place. There are also no cans or plastics to end up in landfills.

If you were able to take it one step further and "go organic" with your meats and vegetables, you would be even greener. If a food is labeled organic, that means it was raised without synthetic herbicides, pesticides, or other chemicals. The production of organic foods creates less pollution in the ground water and soil around us, fewer toxins in the earth, and fewer long-term health consequences for all animals. As reported online in 2007, in Occupational and Environmental Medicine, an international peer-reviewed compilation that is part of the British Medical Journal, several studies conducted in France and the United States have found a definitive causal link between pesticides, herbicides, and fungicides, and cancer in people who work with them on a regular basis. Currently, no long-term study exists that proves the safety of consuming small amounts of those chemicals over a lifetime, either in humans or in cats. So, until there is a clear answer on the safety of conventionally grown foods, it may be a good idea to look for organically grown ones as a carbohydrate and meat source for your kitties.

The difference between "natural" and "organic"

Organic food can only be labeled "organic" in the United States if it meets strict requirements regarding the growing and handling of the item. To be labeled "organic," a food must be free of all chemical preservatives, must have been grown without synthetic fertilizers, and must never have come in contact with man-made pesticides or fungicides.

A governmental body, on the other hand, does not regulate natural foods. The International Association of Natural Products Producers is trying to create some agreed upon terminology. Until that happens, there is only a generalized definition of natural food: something that comes from a plant, animal, or mineral and is not artificially or chemically changed.

Therefore, all organic products are natural, but not all-natural products are organic.

Raw Versus Cooked Meat

Though everyone agrees that cats need their protein, there is some controversy over whether or not it is best to serve them meat that is cooked. Proponents of both sides argue that they have successfully cured their cat's specific disease, alleviated symptoms, and facilitated weight loss with their preferred diet. As you weigh your options and decide what will be best for you and your feline friend — either raw or cooked meat — keep in mind that regardless of which path you take, you must make sure you feed your cat high-quality protein. Hot dogs will not cut it. Neither will processed lunch meats nor the mysterious meat that has been in the bottom of your refrigerator for too long. Your tom or she-cat can get sick eating the same things that would make you sick.

Going raw

Cat parents who insist on feeding their companions only raw foods remind us that many of the nutrients in meat are lost when it is cooked, including the essential amino acids arginine and taurine. They also explain that cooking meat makes the source animals' bones brittle, therefore dangerous for your cat to chew on, whereas raw bones are an excellent source of calcium and they can serve as nature's toothbrush for your cat. Another benefit of feeding your cat raw is one that has nothing to do with nutrition. Many people insist their cats simply prefer raw meat; that they just like the taste of it better than anything cooked. Their argument seems to be backed by cat parents who have successfully trained their cats either for household behavior or to do tricks on command. Apparently, more kitties are apt to respond to the wishes of their pet owners if the smell of raw meat is nearby.

CASE STUDY: RAW FOODS SUCCESS STORY

Robin A. F. Olson
Author, member of the Cat
Writers' Association
info@coveredincathair.com
www.coveredincathair.com

*Robin A. F. Olson is a member of the Cat Writers' Association. In addition to providing entertaining cat stories, her website (**www.coveredincathair.com**) is a helpful resource for cat owners. She is a strong advocate for raw foods as the following success stories show.*

Olson's cat, Bob Dol was given to her after her mother passed away. Bob had only been to the vet once in his life. He was fed low-quality canned and kibble food, and after discovering this, Olsen immediately took him to the vet and learned the health obstacles he faced. He tested positive for feline immunodeficiency virus *(see Appendix for more information on FIV)*, had most of his teeth removed and had diabetes, liver problems, poor coat condition, and low energy. However, that was four years ago. Today, the fact that Bob is even alive was amazing to Olson, but after being put on a grain-free, raw-meat diet, his coat is great, he regained energy, his liver function improved, and the diabetes disappeared.

Olson's second cat, Spencer, had chronic breathing problems resulting in loud wheezing. Olson said she spent thousands of dollars on tests and treatments only to find out he had scar tissue built up in his sinus from an upper respiratory infection he had as a kitten. Today, Olson said you can barely hear him breathe. "The raw diet helped clear up the sinus irritation. His coat is also magnificent, and he is full of life," she said.

Nicky, another tom Olson owned, constantly suffered from urinary tract blockages. "In fact, he almost died from a blockage, most likely from sediment buildup caused by dry kibble," she said. Olson wishes she had been feeding him grain-free then, because she is sure it would have saved her the $8,000 surgery bill to remove his reproductive organs so he could urinate through a bigger opening. Now that he is on raw, she said his rear end, which used to have a gummy residue on it, is nice and clean. "Nicky, who was also obese, has lost a few pounds and looks great," said Olson.

Finally, Olson has a 9-year-old cat that just had blood work completed on her and to the astonishment of Olson's vet, the blood work looked like that of a 2-year-old cat. "The veterinarian knows I feed raw," she said. "I wish he would get on board and start telling his other clients about this!"

Olson said when you see your cats dig into their raw food for the first time, it will really thrill you. "You will be surprised at how they take to it, how they clean their plates, how they have energy they never had before, and how they seem to be more relaxed and less tense," she said. "They are finally getting what they so desperately need, and they lose weight as well." Cats are obligate carnivores, which is an animal whose body physiology makes it difficult to eat and digest plant matter to stay healthy. Olson believes to feed them anything else is a crime.

It can be difficult to transition cats to grain-free and raw foods, and Olson knows it is also more expensive and time consuming to prepare raw food, but with the success she has had with it, she feels the effort is worth it. "Besides, the fact that the cats no longer waste their food and are not getting sick, saves me money," she said. "I would never go back to feeding dry kibble again."

Unfortunately, many veterinarians do not agree with feeding animals raw meat, or they choose to ignore the health benefits. Olson said the only person who supported her feeding a raw diet to her cats was a homeopathic veterinarian.

"I literally had to fight a traditional vet when he diagnosed my cat with diabetes, then told me I should feed a dry kibble or canned food that was full of grain," she said. "When I pushed back and told him that it did not make sense to feed a diabetic cat food with grain in it, he showed me a glossy brochure from a leading pet food manufacturer and said they produced their food in a sanitary environment and that it was tested on other cats, so it must work." When she refused to take the vet's advice about feeding, she said he became offended, but she is sure that she made the right decision for her cat. "After changing my cat to a grain-free diet, within four weeks he was completely off insulin and has not relapsed in four years," said Olson.

Cooking all the way

Proponents for cooking your cat's meat are concerned with the risk of parasitic, bacterial, and viral contaminates that can sometimes be found in raw meat. Though many of those contaminates may be minimally harmful to a healthy tom, they pose particular dangers for a cat with a compromised immune system, an autoimmune disease, kittens relying on a nursing mom, or a senior cat on medication. Some contaminates, such as E. coli and salmonella, are quite dangerous and can even lead to death. Fans of cooked foods also argue that the commercial meat bought in a store is not the same as wild meat. It has already been processed, and so to a certain extent, it has been stripped down from its natural state. Nutritionally, it is not quite the same as wild prey, and often it has been exposed to chemicals and handling that further alters its natural state. Therefore, the belief that you are going raw because you are giving your cat food in its pure and natural form is a false one, according to some.

CASE STUDY: A RAW DIET IS NOT FOR EVERYONE

Cynthia L. McManis, DVM, DABVP
Just Cats
Veterinary Hospital
1015 Evergreen Circle
Woodland, TX 77380
281-261-5555
www.justcatsvets.com

Cynthia L. McManis, DVM, DABVP, has a feline veterinary practice called Just Cats Veterinary Services in Woodlands, Texas. She is a little more cautious when it comes to feeding raw foods to cats.

McManis admits there have been an increased incidence of hyperthyroidism, obesity, and diabetes in cats over the last several years, and nutrition is also most likely related to disease, such as idiopathic, hepatic, lipidosis, and inflammatory bowel disease, but she is quick to point out the role commercial diets play is still under investigation.

She has found there is no objective scientific evidence that feeding raw food is helpful in preventing or controlling diseases, and there are still major safety concerns. Her concerns of a raw food diet include risk of infectious disease, foreign body ingestion (bones), and nutritional inadequacies, as many of the diets on the market are not Association of American Feed Control tested or approved. Of these concerns, infectious disease is probably the biggest. Freezing does not destroy most bacteria, and though irradiation can kill many bacteria, it is not being widely used. Owners using these diets may have risk not only through handling, but also through exposure to pathogens being excreted in the feces of their cats on raw diets, which can be a major concern for immune-suppressed individuals.

In one study of raw food diets, a variety of food poisonings were evident: E. coli was found in 64 percent of the feces, salmonella in 20 percent, Clostridium perfringes in 20 percent, and Staphylococcus aureus in 4 percent.

McManis believes commercial cat foods can be healthy for our cats; in particular, those that are canned, AAFCO approved, and use both nutritional profiles and feeding trials. She recommends feeding different flavors and brands when there are no allergies or sensitivities that preclude variety. This is not to say that she would never feed a raw diet, because she has. However, she screens those clients and cases very closely before recommending raw food.

According to McManis, the biggest challenge cat owners face today — when it comes to feeding their cats nutritionally sound healthy foods — lies in reading and deciphering all the information that they find on the Internet. She believes much of that information is anecdotal and is not evidence-based medicine. Her suggestion would be to engage the cat's veterinarian in discussion and acquire materials from actual research versus literature that has not been peer reviewed.

Most cat owners' lives are fast paced, and they are focused on convenience when feeding. This can be problematic for cats who would be eating six to 12 small meals a day under normal circumstances and getting a great deal of exercise when hunting for their meals. The practice of one or two meals of dry food per day coupled with the sedentary lifestyle of the indoor cat has affected the physical and emotional well being of our feline friends. Also, cats' propensity to mask or hide disease until very late in the process creates problems for owners. The American Association of Feline Practitioners has a plethora of information to help owners recognize health issues in their cats. Coming up with alternate ways of feeding and enriching the environment of cats — particularly indoor cats —requires ingenuity, flexibility, research, and follow through. Creating dialogue with your veterinarian to discuss nutritional and subsequent disease risks and behavioral issues is paramount for the health and well being of all cats.

Making Changes to Your Cat's Diet

Now that you have explored options for creating a healthy menu for your cat and have chosen the direction you want to go, you must seriously consider how you are going to make the necessary changes to your cat's diet. Regardless of whether you are supplementing your cat's commercial food with natural, home-prepared meals or if you are making a radical overhaul of his or her diet to create everything yourself, you must ease into the transition. You must also realize you may have to drag the cat along with you. The most difficult obstacle you will have is not in finding the proper foods, finding the time to prepare them, or finding the storage area in your freezer to keep the foods. It may just be in convincing him or her that it is a good idea.

After all, your tom is a rather particular individual. He has finicky tastes about food and has exacting demands regarding the dining environment. Why on earth would your cat be expected to accept radical changes to his or her diet without putting up a classic feline front? You can make it easier on your cat — and yourself — if you take into account his or her lovable steadfastness, and start slow, go slow, and end slow. Start by offering one new food a day. A one-ingredient food is best, and as animal holistic health practitioner Deb Teubert suggests in her Case Study previously found in this chapter, a dime-sized amount is sufficient. Make those initial attempts to change your cat's diet by first providing something meat-based, something that will appeal to your cat's incredible sense of smell. A spoonful of boiled, chopped chicken livers will make a good first nibble. You can mix it into canned food, or if he or she seems particularly drawn to the smell, try serving it solo in his or her dish. Increase the amount of natural foods each day while weaning him or her off old foods until you have reached your goal of either supplementing commercial foods or replacing them completely.

Junk food addict!

Grunt, a cat in Michigan, was famous in his community for his extreme fondness of potato chips. Whenever anyone in Grunt's family opened a bag of potato chips, he would hear the plastic rumpling and come running. Teenagers in the household resorted to hiding from him in their bedrooms, where they would watch his little paws stretch beneath the door, blindly searching for his favorite treat.

If you are planning on a complete makeover of your cat's diet, going from all commercial foods to all home-prepared meals, you should expect the transition to take anywhere from three weeks to two months, depending on his or her will and digestive system. Smaller cats will need a slower change than larger cats, as their intestinal tract will be even shorter, which gives the food less time to break down, making the cats more prone to discomfort. You should wait to incorporate nutritional supplements, such as omega-3 oils, eggshells, and vitamins, only after you have completely made the switch.

Perhaps the most important thing to remember when making any changes to your cat's diet is to discuss everything with your veterinarian. The veterinarian may want to monitor your cat's progress and may even have suggestions for particular foods or nutrients he or she feels your cat needs. But you should also be prepared for your veterinarian to be concerned about your desire to feed your cat an all-natural diet. The vet will want to be certain you are taking into account your cat's nutritional needs and sensitive gastrointestinal tract as you make changes to his or her diet.

Food reactions

Always stay on the lookout for food reactions. Aside from feline finickiness, you must also remember your cat has a very sensitive digestive system. If he or she exhibits any sort of change in behavior after eating new foods, it may be a sign he or she is not tolerating them well. Signs of an allergic reaction may include swelling around the eyes and difficulty breathing. If your cat is having difficulty digesting the foods, his or her stomach may be bloated, and he or she may act like it hurts when you touch. Other symptoms to look for include rumbling sounds from the abdomen, gas, loose or watery stools, constipation, and lethargy.

If you suspect your cat is having a difficult time digesting the food, and you are sure it is not an allergic reaction, you may consider giving the system a few days to recover before offering it again. The second time, feed him or her less of it.

It may simply have been an issue of trying too much too soon. But sometimes the second time a food is given to an animal, the reaction worsens. If symptoms persist with a smaller amount of food, do not give it to him or her anymore. And of course, if symptoms do not improve, or actually worsen, seek the advice of your veterinarian. Do not think that the cat will quit eating something because he or she is having a problem with it. Some cats will continue to eat a food they cannot tolerate if they like the taste well enough, so you cannot judge their intestinal fortitude by their epicurean behavior.

Preferred Dining Environment

Regardless of what option you choose when feeding your cat, you must make sure he or she has an environment where he or she feels comfortable eating. Cats are not only particular about what goes into their bodies; they are equally fussy — though they deem it as being style conscious — about what is going on around their bodies when they eat. If a cat is stressed or otherwise uncomfortable, he or she will only eat if absolutely starved.

Cats do not like to eat in areas with heavy traffic or loud noises. A mudroom where children are constantly running in and out, tossing shoes and coats about, will be too disruptive for your cat. Your cat will be flinching and on alert instead of focused on food. Similarly, if you have other pets, you may want to put their food dishes in an area away from your cat's, as it goes against the protective instincts to eat at a communal table — or food dish. Finally, cats are like humans, they do not like to eat next to the litter box.

For your cat to be relaxed and at ease enough to eat a healthy meal, he or she needs to have a place where he or she will not feel compelled to look out for other animals or nosy people. Cats are territorial and do not appreciate having to share their little corner of the kitchen; they prefer the area to be theirs to use. In addition, your cat needs to feel safe, trusting that other animals — including well-meaning human animals who are just trying to reach for something on the shelf above her — will not try to take away his or her precious food.

It is even doubly important when introducing new foods to your cat that he or she feels safe and at ease when eating. Your cat's guard may already be up when spotting something that might be "foreign" in his or her dish. If your cat is on edge because the dining environment is not as peaceful and safe as desired, it will only make the transition to a new diet even more difficult.

Cats can be stress eaters

Lisa Clark, a writer in Michigan, owned a cat named Dutchess when she was a child. Dutchess had a long and healthy life, living to be more than 19 years old. She was a self-feeder, that is, her humans would fill her bowl up, and she would only eat whenever she needed to and whatever she needed to. She was sleek and slim and never overate — unless her family left her.

Whenever the Clarks would go out of town for a long weekend, they would fill her bowl to the top, usually with enough food to last a week. But if ever they came home early, they would find she had devoured every morsel, sometimes in less than a day. How she knew their vacation plans they never figured out, but she must have been convinced they were never coming back.

It turns out, the restrained little Dutchess was a big time closet stress eater. Apparently, she could "digest" family travel plans, but had no concept of rationing.

Proper Serving Size and Caloric Intake

Just as with humans, cats get their energy from the calories they consume in their foods. For each gram of protein a cat eats, he or she receives four calories. Your cat will also get four calories from each gram of carbohydrate, but he or she will get nine calories for each gram of fat. A calorie is a calorie, though, and he or she will burn them all off or store all of them in fat, depending on the amount of activity he or she engages in.

The typical adult house cat needs to eat somewhere between 240 and 350 calories per day to have enough energy to pounce, stalk, and sunbathe. You can reduce that number for a customized count for your cat by giving him or her 30 to 35 calories per pound of body weight per day. If your tom is very active, he may need more calories, whereas a sedentary cat, or one already overweight, would need fewer.

The following chart compiled from the National Academies' recommendations details the changing caloric needs for a healthy cat.

Life Stage of Cat	Daily Recommended Caloric Intake	
	5-pound cat	10 to 15-pound cat
Kittens (post weaning)	200	-
Domestic cat	170	280 - 360
Pregnant/nursing mother	336	603 - 851

The above chart reflects the number of calories the average cat needs to consume in order to live happily on a day-to-day basis. However, there are body stressors and environmental influences that may require you to adjust the amount of food your cat eats.

You may notice temperature changes affect the activity level of your cat. An increase in physical activity will increase a cat's body temperature. Therefore, most cats will slow down in the heat, or they risk overheating and suffering from heat stroke. Likewise, they will be a little more spry and energetic in chilly weather, to keep their body temperatures warm enough. If you notice your cat has slowed down due to extended periods of warmer temperature, you will want to lower his or her calorie count to prevent weight gain. On the other hand, if your cat is pouncing and running with more frequency to stay warm in cooler weather, you may want to consider giving him or her more food.

Health status and condition are other considerations that may impact the amount of food you feed your cat. If your adult cat is recovering from surgery or is suffering with a health issue, you may want to either up caloric intake or boost vitamin levels with a supplement. Speak to your veterinarian to see if there is anything you can do to help speed the recovery. And if your cat is exhibiting signs of nervousness or stress — excessive scratching, repetitive behaviors, and staying in hiding — you should probably not expect him or to eat as much as normal.

Regardless of age or stage of life, try to keep in mind that you should give your cat the benefit of doubt when it comes to how much he or she should be eating. Before making any changes to your cat's calorie intake, give him or her a couple of days to see if maybe he or she feels the need to eat more or less food. What you perceive as an increase in activity may just be a temporary, or even momentary, situation that does not require a change diet.

Translating your cat's caloric intake into meals is a little tricky and depends on if you are planning on feeding him or her a diet of raw foods or one of cooked foods. The following table may help clear things up a little. The serving size used on the chart is 1 ½ ounces, which is about one heaping tablespoon of raw meat or 2 ½ tablespoons cooked, as some of the weight and nutrients are lost in the cooking process. Keep in mind the ounce-to-tablespoon conversion is relative and may be different for various meats and fat levels; weighing the food will always be best as it will give a more accurate number. Also, regarding the meats, if you are feeding raw and grinding in the bones, the following calories will actually be lower than what you are feeding your cat. Fat serving size is 1 tablespoon and carbohydrate-serving size is 1 ounce cooked food, which — again depending on food source — is about 1 tablespoon.

Protein/Fat Sources	Calories
Cornish game hen	69
Turkey, ground	40
Chicken, ground mix of light and dark	41
Beef	75
Buffalo and bison	31
Ostrich	47
Emu	31
Venison	34
Goat	31
Lamb	80
Fish, white (species dependant)	25 – 35
Fish, cold-water (species dependant)	50 – 60
Whole, large eggs	75
Guinea fowl	45
Rabbit	39
Quail	54
Pheasant	51
Chicken	178
Beef tallow	115
Fish liver oil	123

Carbohydrate Sources	Calories
Carrots	10.25
Pumpkins	5.75
Sweet potatoes	29.75
Winter squash	11.25
Summer squash	5
Celery	5
Parsnips	23
Peas	23
Green beans	10
Greens (dandelion, collard, etc.)	3.5 – 5
Grasses (barley, oat, rye, wheat)	10 – 15
Rice, cooked	36.5
Rice bran	90
White, skinless, cooked potatoes	25
Whole oats, cooked	17.5

Feeding Through the Ages

As your cat goes from kitten to adult to senior, the food intake and nutritional needs will change. As a kitten, your tabby gets all the food he or she needs from the mother. When your cat is about 4 weeks old, the mother will start the process of weaning and will begin to encourage the kitten to be a little more independent. The weaning process includes learning to eat foods the mother is eating as well as using the litter box and how to socialize and behave in the real word.

Weaning can take anywhere from 2 to 4 weeks of age. The first foods you will want to offer the kitten will be more gruel-like in texture (it should look like watered-down oatmeal) than the food he or she will eat as an adult. The particles of food will need to be small enough to get into his or her tiny mouth, so using a food processor to pulverize the food may be your best option. As your cat gets older, you will be able to use less liquid. By the time your cat is 10 weeks old, he or she will be able to eat food at the same consistency as an adult cat, but you may still need to keep the bite sizes small. However, the 10-week deadline is flexible. If your kitty was premature at birth, he or she may need another few weeks to get used to the chunkier foods. On the other hand, if your cat is hearty and hale, he or she may want to tackle the bite-sized foods a little earlier.

Because of their non-stop play and exploration, kittens do need to eat more frequently throughout the day. They can eat up to six times a day until they are 3 months old. From 3 to 6 months of age, they will be happy to eat four times a day, and by the time they are 6 months old, most are ready to eat just two times as day as a full-grown cat does.

A cat is considered adult at 6 months of age. The nutritional needs outlined in this book will serve him or her well throughout adult life. Like all cats, yours will benefit and attain optimum levels of health from a diet that provides proper nutrition and calories. You can feel comfortable feeding your cat a variety of fresh meats, vegetables, and easily digestible grains, and know that by doing so you will give him or her the nutrients necessary to enhance the quality of life.

Though technically, cats are not considered senior until they are 12, adult cats can begin showing their age as early as 7 years old. It is around that age when some cats start to experience a change in their metabolic rate and the strength of their immune system. You will know because, like humans, your cat's hair may change color, signs of gravity's pull might start to show on the body in a drooping tummy, and your cat may not be as willing to leap to the top of the bookcase as frequently as when he or she was younger. Internal signs may not be as easy to identify, but senior cats are more prone to arthritis, intestinal problems, tooth decay, and tartar buildup.

As your cat ages, you will need to be on your toes and keep an eye out for any change in activity level so you can adjust the calorie count accordingly to maintain a healthy weight. You might also want to speak to your veterinarian to see if you should increase vitamin E intake to help boost antibody levels. Perhaps, you will need to include more antioxidant vitamins in your cat's diet to help fight off free radicals. Unfortunately, most of the foods that are high in antioxidants are fruits, spices, and vegetables cats cannot eat. However, rice bran, oats, leafy green vegetables, broccoli, peas, and pumpkin do contain many antioxidant vitamins. To help with thinning hair, you can add omega-3 fatty acids found in fish liver oil to his or her diet.

Making a complete overhaul of your cat's diet may seem like a daunting task right now — considering the various options you have to choose from for feeding your cat an all-natural diet, trying to figure out caloric needs, and how to change the diet as your cat matures. It all can seem a bit too much at first glance. But, once you make the commitment and start the process, new habits will kick in, and everything will eventually flow as smoothly as it did prior to making any alterations. It probably will not take long before you notice positive changes in your cat. Soon enough, you will know that the effort to modify his or her diet was more than worth it.

Natural Cat Care

· ·

The benefits of a natural diet are generally obvious within a few months, and once cat owners become aware of the positive changes in their cats, it is not unusual for them to start looking at other ways to improve their cat's quality of life. Though cats are low maintenance, they do require more than just food and shelter. There are plenty of opportunities to incorporate natural products, techniques, and ideas into your care for them.

Specific Cat Needs

Cats have particular requirements and needs that must be met not only for their good health, but for their happiness as well. They prefer to have their own private powder rooms, well-manicured nails, comfortable routine dental care, and entertainment that befits their cool and sophisticated taste in toys. The good news is everything can be taken care of with natural products and methods.

The litter box

Perhaps the one area where most cats show their territorial nature is in their littler box. They just do not like to share, but there are also times when they just do not want to use it. Many times, it will be because the placement of the box is in an area with just too much human traffic or activity. Other reasons include the size of the box. In the case of a kitten, the sides of the box may be too high to climb into. You can also check to see if the litter is uncomfortable on his or her paws. If you empty some litter onto the floor, and your cat refuses to step on it, it may be too abrasive. Lastly, your cat may have a urinary tract infection that causes her pain when urinating. Because your cat goes to the box, he or she may associate the litter box with the pain.

If you have tried to remedy all the above techniques and your cat still refuses to use the litter box, it may be because the container has become too odorous. If you cannot replace it, you can try to create your own natural odor remover based on hydrogen peroxide, baking soda, and dishwashing liquid. *See the Recipes Section for complete directions.*

Did you know?

Cats can be trained to use a toilet instead of a litter box.

It takes patience, a bowl large enough to fit inside the toilet, and a willing cat to tolerate the training, but it is definitely possible. You will only need to use the bowl until your cat is completely comfortable, and then you may just need to keep the latest issues of *Cat Fancy* magazine in the powder room. Check out **www.karawynn.net/mishacat/toilet.html** for more details.

Eye care

Some cats are prone to a watery discharge due to tear duct issues. When that discharge is exposed to air, it oxidizes and changes to a brownish color that clings to the eye rim. A number of natural remedies for this condition can be applied with a soaked cotton ball wiped gently over the area or via a dropper. The homeopathic remedy euphrasia tincture, mixed with water is perhaps the most convenient as it is used only once per day. However, other remedies are more easily found at your local grocer. Just three drops of any of the following: Freshly squeezed cucumber juice, chamomile infusion — one teaspoon dried chamomile steeped for a half hour in boiling water then allowed to cool — or cod liver oil can be applied three times a day.

Hair and skin

Most cats believe when they wish to be groomed, their tongue will suffice. If more work is necessary, they will brush off their excess hair onto the darkest trousers or sweaters they can find, and that — really — is all they feel needs to be done. Their human owners, however, disagree and have the audacity to try to brush and groom their cats on a regular basis. To keep hair balls at a minimum, veterinarians suggest shorthaired cats should be brushed quite frequently beginning in late spring and throughout the summer when they are more prone to shedding. Long-haired cats should be brushed year round because they are prone to knots and tangles.

Your tabby will definitely hold a grudge against you should you try just pulling the brush or comb through a knotted chunk of fur. Run your fingers thoroughly through the hair before brushing it to find knots first. If there are any, massage cold-pressed grape seed oil into the knot before trying to de-mat it. Water will only make the hair more resistant, and it may just make your tabby angrier unless he or she is one of the few domestic cats who like water.

Fun Fact

According to **www.catscan.com**, 25 percent of cat owners blow-dry their cats' hair after giving them a bath.

Feeding your cat a healthy diet with plenty of fish oil will go a long way toward keeping your cat's hair and skin healthy. Should the skin condition, dandruff, flare up, you can treat it with a mixture of equal parts vinegar and water applied with a cotton ball and allowed to dry. If it seems like you are feeding your cat plenty of fish oil, but he or she is still showing signs of dandruff, you can add flaxseed oil or ground flaxseeds to the diet, both of which can be found at health food stores and some pet supply stores. As the name suggests, flaxseeds are the seeds of the flax plant, the Linum usitatissimum, which has been used to make paper and fabric for centuries. Flax will not satisfy your cat's nutritional need for omega-3 fatty acids because it does not contain the correct chemical compound, but it still helps with the dandruff. You may also want to check the humidity level in your home, particularly if the dandruff shows up in the winter and your house is being heated with dry air from a central heating unit. If none of the above helps dandruff problems, seek out the advice of a veterinarian. Regardless of what you do, do not attempt to use a human dandruff shampoo. The compounds in that shampoo can be toxic to cats.

Nails

Your cat may love the color and style of your sofa so much that he or she just cannot keep the claws off it. Your cat's affection will run so deep he or she can scratch away the entire left side of your favorite couch and still not be satisfied. Yet, for some reason, even though you have a scratching post that matches the rest of the furniture, he or she does not even give it a casual glace. Before you resort to concrete furniture, you can try rubbing catnip oil onto the scratching post. It just may distract him or her enough to leave your sofa and find a new target. Also, if you do not mind a citrus scent, you could try rubbing lemon or orange essential oils onto the sofa (in a hidden area, as they may stain). Cats usually do not like the aroma of citrus and will stay away from it.

When purchasing scratching posts, you should be sure the post is high enough, at least two feet, to be worthy of being scratched. And carpet-covered posts may not be the best bet. Many of them are covered with less-expensive carpeting, which may emit formaldehyde while he or she is scratching them, so they should be placed in well-ventilated areas. Carpet-covered posts may also encourage him or her to scratch on the similarly textured carpet on the floors of your home. Perhaps finding or creating your own posts covered in sisal or even tree bark would be better alternatives.

You must also remember to trim your cat's claws every couple of weeks. Most owners only clip the front nails, because those are the ones most frequently dug into furniture, legs, and the occasional golden retriever. But the back ones may need to be trimmed on a less frequent basis. So, if it seems your cat is getting his or her back claws stuck in places where they should not be, you may need to give them a trim.

How many toes are on a cat paw?

Cats typically have five toes on their front paws and four on the back. There are some cats, called polydactyl cats, which are born with six or even seven front toes. Ernest Hemingway was famously fond of cats with extra toes. To this day, his home in Key West continues to provide food and shelter to the descendants of his polydactyl cats.

If you wish to try clipping your cat's nails at home instead of taking him or her to the veterinarian, a guillotine-style clipper is best to use. Some owners are fortunate to have cats that slip into a trance-like state when picked up by the scruff of their necks. It is easy to trim the nails of those cats, because they do not move when they are picked up like that. Other cats will need to be held gently, but firmly, when it is time for a trim. Feeding your cat flower essences to make him or her calm before you begin will also help keep it a stress-free time.

It may seem counterintuitive, but if you hold the clippers in a vertical position so that the nail is trimmed from the bottom up, you will get a cleaner cut. Trimming from side-to-side, as humans do, will make the cat's nail more apt to fray and split. Keep stevia liquid extract, a natural artificial sweetener you can buy at all health food stores and most standard grocery markets, on hand in the event of an accidental clip that causes bleeding. Pour some in a small bowl and immediately dip the offended nail into it should a clip occur. The stevia will help stop the bleeding, reduce swelling, and speed up heeling. The Chinese remedy Yunnan Paiyao is equally handy, but harder to find unless you live in a large city with a Chinatown section. You may need to order it online from a specialty store. *See Resources in the Appendix for further information.*

Teeth

You must keep your cat's teeth clean. Periodontal disease — an inflammation of the gums — can result from poor dental hygiene that allows bacteria or tartar to build up on your cat's teeth. Many older cats must be sedated for annual teeth cleaning to remove tartar buildup, but if you start at a young age, you can train your cat to tolerate a good teeth brushing. There are plenty of commercial toothpastes available for your cat. It is imperative you never — ever — use human toothpaste. It is toxic for your cat and can make him or her dangerously ill if some of the paste is swallowed.

To encourage teeth cleaning in your kitten, start by gently and calmly getting him or her used to having a finger massage the gums. Eventually, your cat will allow you to rub his or her teeth. You can introduce a cotton swab dipped in colloidal silver when you feel he or she is ready, and clean the teeth with it. Colloidal silver has antibacterial properties to it that will kill bad germs. When you think your kitten is ready, introduce him or her to the toothbrush, and then the toothbrush with toothpaste on it. Your local pet supply store will carry many styles of brushes and options for paste. You may want to experiment with different brushes to find the one that your tom prefers the most.

Toys

Playtime is an essential part of a cat's life regardless of age. Playing helps keep the body nimble and the mind young; but not all cats like the same toys. Some prefer to drag things along the floor, as if they are captured mice. Some cats like to bat small items back and forth; while others are like human children — they prefer the bag from the pet store to the toy that came in the bag.

You do not need to spend money at a pet store to buy cute toys with artificial eyes and tails. A ball made of wadded up aluminum foil or the ring from a plastic milk jug can be just as entertaining and fun. Some cats love feeling like they are in command of inanimate objects and will delightfully order a pencil to roll across the kitchen floor, yet others will be happy to stalk a shoelace snake as it slithers behind a chair. A toy many cats never tire of is a flashlight. They love to stalk a moving point of light or pounce on it only to discover it disappeared and reappeared in another place.

You will need to be careful of your homemade toys. Cats do like to chew on strings, rubber bands, and holiday tinsel, which can be quite dangerous for them should they swallow any of it. Be sure they do not have access to those items alone. Letting your tabby play in a paper bag is safe and cute, but he or she can suffocate in a plastic bag. Also, should your cat chew a hole in it, the plastic could cause a blockage in the intestines that will only be remedied with surgery and a stint at an animal hospital. Similarly, whatever you use for a toy must be larger than your tabby's mouth. You do not want playtime to end up with a trip to the emergency veterinarian because he or she accidentally swallowed the toy.

How to tell if a cat is happy

Cats have many ways to tell us what mood they are in. Their body language will give us many clues.

A quivering cat tail is supposed to be an expression of deep love and devotion. However, a thrashing tail is a sign of great anger, and a wagging tail is a sign of internal conflict — stay or go?

If your cat is following you from room to room, he or she is feeling sociable and in the mood to be around people. However, if your cat is in stalking position, he or she is either practicing hunting skills or putting them in action.

Your cat's whiskers will also tell you what he or she is feeling. If they are pointing forward and down just a little, you can rest assured that your cat is relaxed and happy. But when they are pointing upward, it is a sign your cat is in an aggressive mood. Additionally, should your cat pull them back against the face, you may want to leave him or her alone, as it is a sign of anger.

It is possible they are trying to connote their feelings by meowing. No one is sure what the meows mean, but an interesting fact is that cats do not meow at each other. It is a behavior they save only for humans, and the more you speak to your cat, the more he or she will "speak" to you.

One more thing to think of regarding your cat's emotions is that he or she is probably keenly in tune with you. Cats have a tendency to read your emotions and adopt them as their own.

The Natural Medicine Cabinet

Without question, a good diet is integral to your cat's health, but there will come a time — or maybe several times — throughout the course of your cat's life when he or she will benefit from an herb or other natural remedy to help heal from the occasional bump in the road of life. Whether for a quick fix for a one-time accidental trauma, or for a repeated need, such as a soothing remedy to help him or her make it through a thunderstorm with little stress, nature provides an assortment of herbs and homeopathic remedies you may want to keep on hand for easy access.

Herbs

Many common herbal medicines and whole herbs can be quite helpful for your cat. In fact, the Veterinary Botanical Medicine Association created a website to help pet owners stay current with herb use and cats. If you check out its website at **www.vbma.org**, you will find the following herbs are considered generally safe for common use, but before you start keeping them on hand in case of emergency, be sure to consult with your cat's veterinarian. He or she may be aware of a specific issue concerning your cat that would have counter implications with a particular herb. Even if given approval by your veterinarian, be sure to watch your cat carefully after each time you administer them for any signs of distress, stomach upset, or potential allergic reaction.

Herbs that improve your cat's immune system include astragalus, echinacea, and American and Siberian ginseng. Astragalus is reputed to have antibacterial, anti-viral, and anti-inflammatory properties. It also increases white blood cell activity to produce antibodies against offending pathogens. Echinacea also increases white blood cells to stave off infection. And both the ginsengs are adaptogenic herbs. They help the body adapt and strengthen to cope with and recover from stress and illness.

Cats who are prone to sinusitis can often benefit from andrographis paniculata and elderberry. For an upset stomach, you can offer fennel, ginger, peppermint, or slippery elm bark *(see Recipes for making an herbal tea)*. Boswellia and cayenne are often beneficial for arthritis and inflammation problems. Goldenseal is considered an antibacterial agent, and arjuna, ginko biloba, hawthorn flowers and berries are all good for heart conditions.

But not all herbs are created equal. You should never give your cat comfrey, red clover, meadowsweet and white willow bark. Those herbs are good for particular human conditions, but they are toxic to your cat. Again, be sure you discuss any herb use with your veterinarian prior to administering it.

Homeopathic remedies

Homeopathic remedies are derived from plant, animal, and mineral sources. The theory behind them is that symptoms can be cured with remedies that cause similar reactions to those symptoms in the body. "Similia similibus curentur" is how the founder Dr. Samuel Hahneman put it back in the 1790s, which means "like cures like." The remedies are chosen based on the symptoms of each individual cat and are sold in potency amounts, instead of grams or milligrams like many other supplements, because the potency is derived by how many times the medicine has been diluted, not by the amount of the medicine. Potency is expressed by the Roman numerals X (for 10), C (for 100), and M (for 1,000) after a number. Hence, a homeopathic remedy potency of 6C is one that has been diluted by 600 times. When looking for a homeopathic remedy for your cat, veterinarians suggest you should choose one whose potency is listed as 30C or lower as a safe place to begin, which should be easy to find in supplement stores, health food stores, and online. Potencies higher than that often can only be found from homeopathic professionals.

If you are completely unfamiliar with homeopathic remedies, it might be a good idea to visit a homeopathic veterinarian for a crash course. Many online companies sell kits of the remedies most frequently used in the common household to help you find what you need out of hundreds of options. You can visit **www.homeopathy.org** for more information on researching appropriate homeopathic remedies and how they work.

Going Green with Cat Care

• •

Feeding your cat an all-natural diet is actually an exercise in being a green, or eco-conscious, human. Hopefully, you will find the experience to be equally rewarding for you as for your cat. Perhaps you will even recognize you are creating a healthier impact on the earth than you used to when you fed your cat processed, prepackaged foods that required heavy industrial methods to create. And, perhaps you may be inspired to expand your greenness even more and try to raise your cat, actually all the animals in the household, in a more environmentally friendly manner. Here are a few tips to get you started.

Recycled pets

The above heading may sound a bit gruesome, but really, it is warm and fuzzy at heart. Every year millions of pets are bought from specialized breeders. Some are bought because the owners need them to be trained for specific work — hunting or herding, for example. Other pets are purchased because the owners have a passionate hobby of showing them in a ring, at a cat show, or even training them for sporting events. All of those reasons are good ones for buying a particular breed from a particular breeder, but most often, people do not buy pets for those reasons.

Most of the time people buy a pet because they want one. They want a hairy, lovable critter to look up at them with adoring eyes. They want a partner to walk with them, to sit in the sun with them, and maybe even to catch that mouse that somehow found its way into the kitchen. If you are one of those people, why buy a pet from a breeder, when you can recycle one from a shelter?

Animal shelters house millions of unwanted pets. And you will even find purebred cats at them. Many of them are young kittens that were born to feral cats or born to the pets of humans who just do not have the financial means or time to care for baby animals. Others at the shelter are pets whose owners had to move, lost their jobs, or became ill, and therefore, unable to care for them.

The animals in shelters are just as capable of being trained as purebred animals. They are just as willing to love and be loved, and they are just as healthy, too. In fact, some people believe that Darwin's law of survival of the fittest actually applies to mixed breeds. For example, Himalayans and other breeds with short noses seem to suffer from sinus issues and even certain brain cancers at higher rates than other cats.

By adopting cats from shelters, you are helping those shelters save on energy resources and cut back on their needs for commercial products they need to feed and maintain them. And you are being a steward for the creatures you share the earth with. Being green means you take as much responsibility as you can for the health and benefit of the entire earth, which includes the unwanted animals living out their lives in the cages of an animal shelter.

Some potential pet owners may balk at the idea of getting a pet from a shelter.

They are afraid that they may end up getting stuck with an ill-behaved or even dangerously aggressive animal. However, most shelters, if not all, will take an animal back if it winds up not being a good fit for the adoptive family. Also, when shelters take an animal in, they get as much history of it as they can. After all, shelters are in the process of saving an animal and finding a better quality of life. They are committed to making sure animals get into happy homes and will work with you to help you find the best animal for your situation.

Reasons for giving up a cat

The National Council on Pet Population Study and Policy tracks and ranks the reasons why animals are taken to shelters. According to their statistics, only two reasons are due to negative behavior being exhibited by an animal.

Here are the top ten reasons why people in the United States give a cat up to a shelter:

1. Too many cats are living in the house.

2. Human in house developed an allergy to cats.

3. The family is moving.

4. The cost for the animal's upkeep was too expensive.

5. The owner was renting, and the landlord insisted no cats were allowed.

6. The cat is the kitten from a litter that the owner just could not find another home for.

7. The cat was "spraying" or peeing throughout the house and would not stop.

8. There were personal issues that developed within the family, and no one was able to care for the cat adequately.

9. The family was unable to provide appropriate facilities for the cat.

10. The cat did not get along with other animals in the household.

Animal shelters, clearly, are a fabulous way to be a green pet parent. And sometimes a pet hero, as when shelters run up against budgetary issues, they may have to resort to putting an animal down, or euthanasia. If you are still on the fence about adopting an animal from a shelter, here are a few questions you can ask to clarify how they receive the animals and any potential problems they may be aware of:

1. When people drop off an animal, do you do anything to find out about its health and behavior history? May I see it?

2. Do you know if this animal gets along well with small children or other animals?

3. Did you or do you know if this animal has been treated for any particular health conditions?

4. Is this animal spayed or neutered?

If you have a penchant for a particular breed of animal and cannot find that breed at an animal shelter, you can still be green and get a recycled pet that fits your wants. Most breeds have rescue groups. They are made of volunteers who are fans of a particular kind of dog and cat to the point that they are willing to take them in and provide a foster home should the need arise. Usually, these animals must be given up because the owner was transferred out of state, became too ill to care for it properly, or had some other major lifestyle change. Often, cats in such foster care will have full paperwork proving their heritage as well as complete medical histories documented.

Spaying and Neutering

Often, when you adopt an animal from a shelter, and even sometimes when you buy one from a breeder, before the pet is relinquished to you, you must agree to spay or neuter it. That simple medical procedure has many benefits for the animal, for you, and (perhaps surprisingly) for the planet. Spayed and neutered animals often live longer lives because they are less prone to succumb to diseases and cancers of the reproductive organs, which is good for the cats. And it is good for you because you get to keep your perky kitty longer, and the veterinarian bill of a spaying or neutering is much cheaper than one covering the costs of cancer.

At this point, you may be asking yourself, "how is spaying and neutering good for the planet?" Well, according to the American Humane Association, it just takes two cats and their offspring, all producing two average-sized litters a year with just two or three kittens from each surviving, to produce 80 million cats. Read that sentence again. It is a staggering amount of animals that will need to be taken care of — with resources that impact the earth to create food, kitty litter, vaccines, and provide shelter and transportation when necessary.

Besides, if your pet has a genetic mutation or a genetic predisposition toward particular illnesses or conditions, unless you neuter him, he is at risk of passing that gene on and weakening future generations. Obviously, the above example shows you how many cats that can impact. But, if you have a tom, it can be even more. There is no limit to how many kittens a tom can sire.

The sheer number of unwanted animals on the planet creates a huge antienvironmental impact. Stray dogs and cats survive by feeding on whatever prey they can find, which can upset the natural balance of an ecosystem. You may not like mice and rats in your homes, but they go to great lengths keeping insects and other pests in control. In urban areas, feral cats soon learn how to tackle garbage receptacles and trash cans, tipping them over or otherwise spilling out their contents. The dogs and cats are completely unaware of the dangers associated with litter clogging up the earth — that plastic bags can escape into waterways and wetlands where they are accidentally ingested by fish and birds, killing them off. And the bacteria in the urine and feces of those wild animals can get into the soil and groundwater where those pathogens can affect other animals, including humans.

Controlling Overconsumption and Packaging

Perhaps the toughest thing to do to be a green pet parent — as well as a green human being — is cutting back on the great American tendency to overconsume. Your need to provide every toy, every gadget, everything for your cat obviously results in an overuse of gas to go out and purchase those items. But, what you may not realize is, anything made from plastic is a petroleum product or by-product. All the shrink-wrap packaging, clear "windows" on boxes, often the items themselves, and the plastic bags you take them home in required massive amounts of refining, pollution, and oil to create and transport to the store. And the thing is, you do not even know if your cat will like it.

There are other, greener options. For example, you can attach a string to a ruler, you can make balls out of used (but clean) aluminum foil, and the list is endless. But toys are not the only items where you have more eco-aware options available.

If you decide to purchase a bed or mat for your kitty, look carefully at the materials. Are they man-made? Or do they come from nature? If it is not cotton, wool, or some other one- or two-syllable word you have known all your life, it is probably synthetic. Polyesters, nylon, and many other man-made fabrics come from, you guessed it, petroleum by-products. For bedding, toys, feeding bowls, even collars, try to purchase items for your cat that are more natural. Bamboo, hemp, organic cotton, or other fabrics and recycled materials are all-sustainable and renewable green products. Most likely, the manufacturing of those items will have required fewer industrial resources and less petroleum, hence is kinder to the planet.

Sustainable or renewable?

When trying to be a green cat parent, you will need to look for products labeled "sustainable" or "renewable" to be sure they are green and eco-friendly. Those words mean that the resources used to create the product came from materials that are easy and quickly replaced. Anything made of bamboo, for instance, is renewable because it grows so very quickly and easily, using it does not leave a lasting scar on the planet. On the other hand, something made of mahogany wood, is not as renewable, as it takes bamboo only a small amount of time to reach maturity, but it can take a mahogany tree decades.

Sustainable materials are not only easy and quick to grow; they often do not need much synthetic treatment in their development, as they usually are plants growing in their native land where it is well adaptive. And other materials, such as cotton, can be sustainable if they are grown organically.

You can now easily find cat toys, bedding, grooming products, and even litter made with sustainable or renewable materials in your local pet supply stores.

More on Toxins

By now, you are aware of the many issues arising from when a cat eats something it should not have. Not only are there a number of grains and vegetables your cat cannot have, but it seems the world is full of potential toxins for her to eat. You may even be considering building a bubble to protect him or her. The good news is that a bubble may not be necessary if you can incorporate more green habits into your lifestyle, hence into his or her home.

According to the Environmental Working Group, more than 80,000 chemicals have been introduced to the world since the 1940s. The explosion in chemistry (no pun intended) happened to coincide with a seeming abundance of, you guessed it, petroleum. What on earth could be done with it? Scientists thought, pondered, and came up with a multitude of ideas. Now those chemicals can be found in soap, shampoo, and other personal care items. They are in our air fresheners, our scented body wipes, and the trash bags with an "odor shield." Petroleum by-products are often the key ingredients in the laundry detergent, fabric softener, dish soap, glass cleaner, toilet cleaner, shower cleaner ... the list is seemingly endless.

Not only are all those products based on the petroleum industry (and do not forget that they are packaged often in non-recycled plastic containers), but also they are toxic to your cat. Even if your tabby is the rare cat that has never been curious enough to wander under the kitchen sink, he or she is still in danger of accidentally ingesting the products you store there. If your cat ever wanders across the kitchen floor while it is damp with tile cleaner, the product can stick to her paws, only to be groomed off later by her detail-oriented tongue and ingested. The same goes for the counter cleaner, the rug shampoo, and possibly even the suntan lotion that has your legs shiny while your cat sits on your lap trying to tell you he or she would rather be inside in the air conditioning.

Using natural products will help lower the potential toxic danger in your house, and not just for your cat. Organizations such as Healthy Child Healthy World (**www.healthychild.org**) are concerned about the continued exposure of children to small quantities of those products throughout their growing lifetime. Children, like animals, can absorb toxins through their skin and breathe them into their lungs. No one has ever tested the majority of the products at all, and no one has ever been able to say without a doubt that they are perfectly safe for children to be exposed to. So, if no one knows for sure how safe they are to use around our children, no one knows how safe they are to use around our pets.

People only had natural products to clean with prior to the 1940s, and they managed to have clean houses, so it is definitely possible to do so now. Green cleaning products are starting to become commonplace. You are now able to find them in just about every grocery store and discount department store.

And traditional cleaning companies seem to be happy to go on board with the demand. Even the makers of Clorox bleach now have a natural, eco-friendly line.

The least toxic cleaners are the ones made from plants, plant products, or naturally occurring enzymes. The label on the bottle should tell you why the product is considered green or eco-friendly. But you do not necessarily have to purchase the products. Baking soda and vinegar have been used for years to clean and even scour homes. Castile soap, a liquid plant-based soap you can find in your local drug store, can also be mixed with water and baking soda to create an effective, and non-toxic, cleaner.

If your cat is not an indoors-only kitty, you should also look in your garage and around the yard for ways to be a greener cat parent. Antifreeze is a common poison for pets, but even if you live in cold climate, you have an effective alternative. There is a product, Sierra Antifreeze, which is safer for the environment and safer for animals than traditional antifreeze. It is now available at many chain hardware and auto supply stores across the United States. For more information on Sierra Antifreeze and stores that carry it, visit the website at **www.sierraantifreeze.com**.

While you are in the garage and thinking about antifreeze, you may think about winter, which may make you think about de-icing supplies. Though you rely on them to clear our driveways and sidewalks of ice and snow, many of the de-icers contain chemicals that are harmful to children and pets, can kill your grass, and even make their way into your drinking water. They are simply not green or environmentally friendly at all. There are, however, plenty of alternatives at your local hardware store. The product label will clearly state how safe it is for animals, but you will also know by looking at the price. Those products can be more expensive. It might be a good idea to stock up on them during the springtime. Often at the end of the winter season, the stores are looking to make space for warm-weather items, so they put the de-icers on sale in an effort to hurry them out the door.

If you do any kind of lawn maintenance yourself, you probably store all of your supplies in your garage as well. So, while you are checking out the antifreeze and de-icers, peek at the chemicals you use to kill weeds, insects, and maybe even mammals. If your cat ever goes outside, he or she will be walking, rolling and lounging in those chemicals on your lawn. For every chemical-laden product, there is an organic or otherwise green one on the market that will be less toxic for your tom and friendlier on the world.

Cat owners must fill many roles, the primary one being the provider of safe shelter, good food, and clean water. Anything beyond that is an added bonus for your cat and maybe even the planet. Clearly, going green can be an extension of your cat-care habits, but it is not a requirement for being a cat owner. Consider the concepts discussed in this chapter, and decide which would be easy to incorporate into your lifestyle and which would be most beneficial for your cat. The next chapter will focus on providing healthy food that can seemingly provide relief for your ailing feline.

CHAPTER
7

Your Cat's Diet as Medicine

• •

No animal's body, including a cat's, can be healthy and thrive with poor nutrition. Feeding your cat a diet chock full of the nutrients and calories it needs will support her body's immune system, which is the primary defender against all disease and parasitic and fungal infections. You are the secondary defender in the way you provide a clean, safe environment, and proper nutrition for her.

The Immune System

Providing good nutrition with quality foods will make your cat's immune system better able to stave off bacterial and viral attacks and heal wounds successfully and efficiently. If you were able to look at your tabby's immune system in a tangible way, you would see that it was neatly divided into two sections. The first is the skin, or innate immune system. The basic job of the skin is to keep everything unhealthy out of the body. It serves as a fortress or wall-type barrier to keep foreign antigens (bacteria, viruses, fungi, and insects) from getting to the interior tissues and organs. In addition to the skin, your cat's saliva, stomach acid, nasal mucus, and specific cells in the blood are parts of the innate immune system. Together, they form the first line of defense against an attacking antigen.

The other part of the immune system is called the adaptive immune system. Adaptive is the key word, because this system looks at an invader and changes, or adapts the body's defenses to specifically target the antigen. Each time the adaptive immune system kicks into high gear, it retains a memory of whom or what the enemy was, so that the next time that particular antigen attacks, the body can fight it off faster and stronger than it did the first time. Now, you know what it means when people say you are "boosting your immune system" with each cold or virus you get — immune systems grow stronger and more capable of fighting off antigens with each attack.

Diet's role in immunity

Many veterinarians, particularly holistic and homeopathic vets, realize the important role diet plays in creating and supporting a strong immune system in your cat. Fresh foods — particularly, raw foods — have higher amounts of nutrients than prepackaged and processed foods. Even the high-quality commercial cat foods cannot compare with freshly made food for your cat. Like all animals, your cat's body has a miraculous capacity to extract vitamins and minerals from food and turn them into soldiers on active duty to repair, heal, and fight off enemy germs and bacteria. If the nutrition in those foods is not naturally present, but instead is manufactured, many holistic professionals believe it is harder on the body to find and use it.

Antioxidants are perhaps the most active nutrients in foods when it comes to supporting and boosting the immune system. The most easily available antioxidants are vitamins A, C, and E, and seem to be the fashionable supplement these days with suppliers offering their version of the nutrients for human consumption in every market and online store. They work in the body by helping cells become more disease resistant. They help keep the liver strong so that it can work at optimum efficiency levels to detoxify the body. And they play an integral role in cell growth. They work by neutralizing the free radicals that build up inside the bodies of cats, and all living animals.

The gastrointestinal tract and immunity

Holistic veterinarians stress that a cat must have a healthy gastrointestinal tract for optimum immune system strength. Its size — a small intestine in an adult cat can be 60 inches long, several times longer than your cat's body — offers a clue as to how important it is in your cat's health. The small intestine is where most of the nutrients, water, and electrolytes from food are absorbed into the bloodstream. If there is any evidence of inflammation or digestive disorders present in your cat's body, he or she will be unable to properly break down the food ingredients and assimilate the vitamins and minerals, therefore he or she will be prone to malnutrition, which will only encourage more inflammation and even disease.

The other job of the intestinal tract is to be on the front line of defense against pathogens. Along with the respiratory system, the gastrointestinal tract is one of the first places where pathogens and bacteria get introduced into the body (whatever goes into the mouth gets into the gut). Again, the sheer size of the intestine magnifies its ability to provide lymphocytes (infection-fighting cells). Therefore, you could say a vast portion of the immune system is housed there, primed and ready to greet the offending bacteria.

Exercise impacts immunity

When cats run, jump, climb, or attack your pen as you write at your desk, they are exercising. Without question, exercise helps keep your kitty stay skinny, which in essence boosts the immune system. It has been proven over and over again that obese animals are more prone to disease and infections than average weight animals. Aside from weight, exercise also strengthens the lungs and cardiovascular system, both of which are instrumental in the innate immune system.

Supplements and herbs to boost immunity

Nutritional supplements may only be a necessary ingredient in your cat's diet if he or she is not getting the proper nutrition needed. But, even if your cat is eating a diverse assortment of fresh meats and carbohydrates, there may be times when her immune system could use a strengthening boost from added vitamins, minerals, or herbs that are antioxidant in nature. If something is an antioxidant, that means it prevents the oxidation of free radicals within the body. Free radicals are a natural by-product in the body. They are atoms or molecules that roam the body looking for extra electrons to take from other cells. Excessive amounts of them are created when the body is trying to fight off the effects of pollution, toxins (including pesticides in foods), stress, or disease. Antioxidants halt the attempts of free radicals to steal electrons from healthy cells, weakening the good cells, thus weakening the body. A healthy body with adequate levels of antioxidants can deal with the constant barrage of naturally occurring free radicals. But, when the onslaught becomes overwhelming because too many free radicals are produced for antioxidants in the body to handle, the result is cell mutation and immune system damage, leading to such dangerous health conditions as cancer, autoimmune diseases, and other illnesses.

If you are feeding your cat a properly balanced diet and supplementing with a good multivitamin, taurine, and calcium, his or her nutritional needs will definitely be met to support the typical cat immune system. However, if she has suffered from a long-term illness, parasitic infection, respiratory infections, or other chronic illnesses, she may need help from herbs and mushrooms to help get her immune system functioning at full speed again. Cat's claw, echinacea, and the Chinese herb astragalus are commonly used to enhance immune system function. Green tea contains compounds called polyphenols that are reported to destroy cancer cells as well as free radicals. Remember, though, that your cat cannot tolerate caffeine, so be sure to use decaffeinated green tea. The Indian spice turmeric is also a very powerful anti-inflammatory herb as well as an antioxidant.

Aside from herbs, shiitake, reishi, and maitake mushrooms, also stimulate killer T-cell production — the blood cells that are part of the innate immune system. And the Chinese mushroom Cordyseps is known for its antioxidant and antiviral properties. Mushrooms can be highly allergenic, though. You must be sure your cat can tolerate them prior to using them as immune-boosting agents.

Addressing Specific Health Conditions

A diet of high-quality natural ingredients will go a long way toward getting and keeping your cat happy and healthy. In fact, many veterinarians, again particularly holistic veterinarians, believe the key to a healthy cat lies in his or her diet. Most will also tell you that even if a cat already has a health condition, he or she can probably regain health faster with a diet custom-tailored to his or her particular situation.

What you feed your cat can influence the following health conditions and probably more. At the end of this book, there are guidelines for changing up the recipes to best accommodate your cat's individual needs. Though it cannot be stressed enough, the recommendations here are only guidelines. You must discuss all dietary changes you intend to make with your cat's veterinarian.

Hair balls

Cats are famous for their self-care. Perhaps they indulge in the calming and cleansing of self-grooming because humans have yet to get around to inventing feline spas, but it is more likely that cats groom themselves for a variety of health reasons that have nothing to do with self-indulgence or looking good. For one, cat specialists believe the licking helps a cat regulate body temperature, meaning that the cat cools down as the saliva evaporates from his or her body.

Grooming also allows your cat to mask his or her presence from other cats or from larger predators by licking away any odors or scents picked up from the environment. The rough, bristly hairs on a cat's tongue helps distribute protective oils around the body and even improves circulation by promoting blood flow at the skin's surface.

The downside to all that grooming is your cat can and will get hair balls. Most cat owners are familiar with finding a ball of hair that their cat regurgitated, usually on the better carpet. The frequency of the hair balls may depend on the season or even geographic location, but at some point, all cats with hair will suffer from them. Trouble passing hair balls can suggest your cat needs more fiber in his or her diet. It can also suggest other more serious problems, such as an intestinal blockage, so be sure to check with your cat's veterinarian before you simply increase the fiber in his diet.

If the veterinarian does feel that more fiber in your cat's diet will help with hair ball issues, you can try feeding him cat grass which you can find at local plant nurseries, some pet supply stores, and even at some natural foods stores. There are various cat grasses available, but oat grass is perhaps the most popular. Although, other cats prefer to chew on wheat and rye grasses, so you may need to experiment to see which one your kitty likes best. All grasses are fibrous, which means they are not easily digestible. Once in the intestines, they will absorb water and soften. The stools will then bulk up and carry out the hair and other non-digestible particles when they pass.

Grow your own cat grass in a flowerpot

There are a couple different options available to you if you want to try your hand at growing grass for your cat. Perhaps the simplest thing you can do is to order a kit. Wheat Grass Kits (**www.wheatgrasskits.com**) is one website where you will find the seeds, the planting medium, the container, and all the instructions you will need to successfully grow wheatgrass for your kitty.

Some health food stores and neighborhood plant nurseries always carry grasses potted in plastic cache pots. You will need to transplant the grass into a larger, more stable terra cotta pot. If you prefer to use plastic, find a larger pot and put heavy rocks or bricks in the bottom to help it stay upright in case your tom is a vigorous muncher or enjoys pretending he is a wild tiger in the jungle, pouncing on prey from behind a giant bush. You will need to transplant the grass as you would any normal houseplant: Put enough potting soil in and around the plant so that the base of the plant remains about an inch below the rim of the pot. Do not compact the soil as you put it into the pot, but you also do not want it to be too loose. Press it down around your plant so that the grass does not shift or fall over when you water it. However, if you find the water pooling at the top of the soil, you pressed too hard and will need to loosen it up and maybe even take some out.

Keep your grass in a sunny spot and water once or twice a week to prevent the soil from drying out and the tips of the plant from turning brown. You can leave it out for your cat to chew when he feels the need. Just remember that it will count as part of the carbohydrate portion of his diet. However, if he tends to be a non-stop nibbler, you may need to take it away to keep him from eating too much of it.

Not all cats are grass fans though, so instead of offering it, you may need to increase the fiber portion of the carbohydrates in his meal. Pumpkin, celery, and summer squashes are good sources of fiber that are also low in calories. Remember, total carbohydrates should only be between 5 and 10 percent of your cat's diet. Anymore than that and you risk stomach distress and weight gain.

Pest control

Fleas are a true pest to cats. Not only do their bites cause an uncomfortable itch for your tabby, they can also cause a host of other problems. Kittens with flea infestations are at risk of anemia and even death. The saliva the flea leaves behind on the bite can cause severe allergic reactions in the cat, making her scratch excessively, leading to hair loss and scabby skin. And cat fleas carry the larvae of *Dipylidium caninum*, (otherwise known as tapeworm). Should your kitty eat one accidentally while grooming, it may just infest her with the tapeworm, which will make her lose weight and suffer other health conditions requiring medical treatment.

Fleas mostly appear in the warm summer months, but they can be yearlong problems. Larval fleas can completely develop into adults and live in their watertight pupal casings up to a year, waiting for the right moment to hatch. Fleas have an uncanny ability to sense the vibrations from a cat moving, smell the carbon dioxide of a cat's breath, and feel the body heat of a nearby cat. When they sense a host animal, they escape their pupal casings and use their super-flea ability to jump and land in the right place at the right time.

Once it makes itself at home on your cat, the flea feeds at leisure and breeds at a rapid pace. Fleas can start breeding their first day of life. To be mature enough to breed simply requires a flea to find a food source first. A female flea then begins laying eggs within two days after breeding and will continue to lay eggs every day of her life. The typical lifespan of a flea is anywhere between one to three months, and an adult flea can lay up to 50 eggs a day, so this means one flea can produce more than 10,000 eggs in its lifetime.

If you find your cat is scratching repetitively, it could be because he or she has fleas. It could also be a sign of other infections or not getting enough essential fatty acids, so a close inspection of the skin and hair should be conducted. Part the hair so you can see clear down to the skin. If fleas are present, they will try to keep hidden in the hair. You will see them moving and jumping away from you, but staying on the animal. The most common area to find fleas will be in the rump and groin area of your cat as they are the places she finds most difficult to scratch. Another way to determine if your kitty has fleas is to take a damp, white towel and rub it vigorously on his or her rear end — caution, your cat may not appreciate the activity and will let you know with equal vigor. Perhaps you should find a willing assistant to help restrain and reassure your cat while you check for fleas. If there any dark specks or smears of a dark, reddish color land on the towel, they could be flea feces.

At this point, you may be wondering why you are reading about fleas in a book on cat nutrition and recipes for cat food. It is a long held belief among holistic veterinarians that fleas prefer weaker hosts, which may explain why younger kittens, whose immune system is not yet fully developed, seem to be more prone to flea infestation than adults. Those veterinarians suggest the first line of defense against fleas is to boost your cat's immune system by adding antioxidant supplements to his or her diet and to increase essential fatty acids to help the skin stay its healthiest and strongest. Nupro Cat Supplements and Animal Essentials are two good sources, but do be sure to discuss with your cat's personal veterinarian to ensure he or she agrees with your decision.

Obesity and diabetes

Wild and feral cats that naturally eat a diet that is high in protein and low in carbohydrates do not get diabetes and generally do not become overweight. In contrast, it is estimated that one in every 400 domestic cats suffers from diabetes, approximately 80 percent of which is from type 2 diabetes. The difference between type 1 and type 2 diabetes in cats is the same as in humans. Type 1 occurs due to a virus or autoimmune disorder. With this type of diabetes, the body becomes unable to produce insulin, the hormone necessary for the transfer of sugar from the blood to the cells. Type 2 diabetes occurs in two ways — when the body produces insulin but is inefficient in the transferring process, or when the body just cannot produce enough insulin.

Many veterinarians believe the difference in the rate of diabetes between wild and domestic cats can be explained by diet, particularly by the amount of carbohydrates those cats eat. When a cat digests food, the body takes the protein, fat, and carbohydrates eaten and converts them into blood sugar, which is also called glucose. As the glucose enters the bloodstream, the pancreas will kick into action and produce insulin. The insulin is supposed to tell the cells to make energy out of the blood glucose or store it for later. The pancreas regulates the production of insulin to match the amount of glucose in the cat's bloodstream for just the right amount of energy to sustain him or her during the day.

Again, type 2 diabetes occurs when a cat cannot produce enough insulin in the pancreas to enable the blood glucose to be metabolized effectively, or when the pancreas does make the right amount of insulin, but it does not make it into the bloodstream. In either case, if the insulin does not make it into the cells, they will lack the energy to function at full capacity, and the insulin will build up in the blood. Often, the first sign of type 2 diabetes is excessive thirst and urination as the cat's body will try to clear itself of the sugar through urination. The excessive urination will then cause an excessive thirst. A diabetic cat will resort to any means of finding more water. Cat owners have reported their cats waiting in bathtubs for water drops to fall from a tap or lurking around the kitchen sink waiting to lap up any overspray.

A diabetic cat will also experience sudden weight changes. He or she may become thinner or may gain weight. Either way, his or her appetite will become insatiable. In addition, an owner might notice a wobbliness to the cat's gait. The back legs will become weaker, in a condition called peripheral neuropathy, a weakening of the nerves in the legs. In diabetic humans, the condition is often seen in the feet. As the disease progresses, an owner may notice a thinning of the cat's skin, which could be a sign that the body is breaking down or metabolizing his or her own body fat and muscle in an attempt to survive. Eventually, if left untreated, a diabetic cat lapses into comas and could die.

The good news is that type 2 diabetes can be treated and even brought to a state of remission through a change in a cat's diet. The suggestion of getting your cat's veterinarian on board with any diet changes is particularly true and imperative when dealing with a diabetic cat. If you change your cat's diet, you must do so under the direct supervision of a veterinarian. Great care must be taken when making changes to a diabetic cat's diet because the veterinarian will need to change the dosage of insulin as the food change occurs. Insulin must be lowered in accordance to the lowering of carbohydrates; otherwise, you risk a dangerous imbalance of insulin and an exacerbation of diabetic symptoms.

A high-protein diet is beneficial for a diabetic cat because of the way he or she digests food. Because protein and fat take a longer time to be broken down than carbohydrates, their conversion into blood sugar happens at a slower rate over a longer period. The extension of the process allows the pancreas to systematically pump out a small amount of insulin over the course of the day, instead of one dumping as happens when the cat eats a large amount of easily converted carbohydrates. Hence, with protein and fat in the diet, a more stable level of blood sugar is then present in the body. Carbohydrates, on the other hand, are converted very quickly. When a cat eats carbohydrates, a large amount of sugar immediately travels into the blood stream. The pancreas must match the effort and produce a larger amount of insulin, which then results in a burst of energy followed by a lengthy lag time.

To feed your cat a high-protein diet, follow the guidelines discussed in Chapter 1, aiming at the higher amounts for protein and lower amounts for carbohydrates — 65 percent protein, 30 percent fat, and 5 percent carbohydrates. You should stick to what are considered low-glycemic carbohydrates for that 5 percent portion. Low-glycemic foods are processed by the body at a slower rate than high-glycemic foods and help prevent a large rush of sugar to the blood stream. Foods that are low-glycemic include grasses, leafy green vegetables, such as kale, Swiss chard, collard greens, and dandelion greens. Celery and other non-starchy vegetables are also good sources of low-glycemic carbohydrates. You should never feed a diabetic cat cooked potatoes or grains because they are higher on the glycemic scale and will cause instant peaks in their blood glucose levels, which will stress the pancreas.

Good, soluble fiber seems to reduce the need for insulin in the human body. You may want to discuss the option of offering your cat a soluble fiber supplement with his veterinarian. Psyllium husk, the seed covering of the plant Plantago psyllium has a long history of being used to add fiber into the human diet and can also be used with some cats. You can find it in powder form in most health food stores and mix it with water, if your cat can tolerate it. Try it in very small amounts at first to see if it causes your cat's stomach any distress. If your cat can tolerate it, do remember to cut back on other vegetables and grains in his or her diet to keep the carbohydrate ratio between 5 to 10 percent of his or her diet range.

If you are supplementing your diabetic cat's high-quality commercial foods with home-prepared natural ones, you will need to read labels carefully. Most of the dry cat foods and kibble are high in carbohydrates and will need to be ignored. If you use canned cat food, you will want to make sure that it derives less than 10 percent of its calories from carbohydrates and that grains are not listed in the ingredients. Not all commercial cat foods list the caloric breakdown for carbohydrates, so you will need to do the math equations discussed in Chapter 4, or you may need to check the manufacturer's website. And remember, most treats and moist cat foods have high carbohydrate content as well. Keeping the carbohydrates low will help keep your cat trim and will help stave off diabetes.

Lower urinary tract disease

A variety of health conditions affecting a cat's urethra and bladder are collectively called lower urinary tract disease. Despite the fact there are numerous conditions under that name, they usually manifest in the same symptoms. Cats suffering from a lower urinary tract disease often exhibit pain when urinating, there may be blood in the urine, and they might start urinating more frequently. Sometimes cats will start to urinate outside the box, often on a tile floor, in a bathtub, or on another cool, flat surface, as they mistakenly associate the pain with using the litter box. Other cats will begin to obsessively lick their genital area.

Some of those symptoms can also be indicative of other conditions. A cat stressed by a new member of the family or other household change may urinate outside the litter box — as will one who does not like where her box is located. Frequent urinating is associated with a variety of illnesses and diseases. Genital licking could also be an attempt to sooth an area infested with fleas. The list could go on indefinitely. Again, discuss any changes in your cat's behavior with your veterinarian to be sure what is causing it.

If your cat is diagnosed with a lower urinary tract disease, there could be several environmental influences causing it or exacerbating it. Cats that are overweight or get little exercise, as well as cats that stay strictly indoors, are more prone to suffering from urinary tract disease. A cat that has a diet of only dry kibble without enough moisture is more likely to suffer from the disease, also. Stressed cats can suffer from a particular lower urinary tract disease called interstitial cystitis that causes bladder pain when urinating. Interstitial cystitis is also suspected when the above symptoms for lower urinary tract disease are present with no obvious cause or reason for them.

A key to keeping your cat's urinary tract in good health is to ensure its body pH, hence its urine pH, is acidic and not alkaline. The term pH refers to the amount of hydrogen there is in a particular substance. Hydrogen levels are what determine whether something is acidic or alkaline. Urine whose pH range falls between 6.0 and 6.5 is considered acidic. You can purchase pH test paper in health food stores, but it is quite difficult to make your cat urinate on them. Instead, a good way to ensure your cat's body stays within that acidic pH range is with through his diet. Meat protein is the best food to encourage acidic urine. Most carbohydrates encourage alkaline urine.

Diet plays a key role in many lower urinary tract diseases, particularly with struvite urinary stones. If a cat's diet contains too much magnesium or is too alkaline, he or she may develop struvite stones, which are hardened mineral deposits, in urine. For such a cat, eliminating all fish from his or her diet will help lower magnesium levels, and decreasing the vegetable carbohydrates in food will make his or her urine less alkaline. Winter squash is one of the few plant foods that can be fed to your cat to help make his or her urine more acidic. Gizzards from chicken and turkey (particularly raw gizzards) are high in the amino acid, L-methionine, which will have an acidifying effect on urine as well.

Diet may play less of a role if the stones are of calcium oxalate — the most common type of kidney stone in humans. It is possible that a deficiency in calcium may lead to calcium oxalate stones, but research is ongoing and inconclusive as of yet. Only a veterinarian who has studied the X-rays of your cat will be able to determine the kind of stone and the course of treatment.

Regardless of which type of urinary tract infection your cat may be suffering from, a key issue regarding lower urinary tract health for cats is the cat's weight. Overweight cats are at an increased risk of suffering from any sort of lower urinary tract issue than cats at a healthy weight. To compound the issue, once an overweight cat develops a urinary tract disease, odds of it recurring rises even more. Should your overweight cat develop a lower urinary tract disease, it is imperative upon his recovery, that he is put on a diet. Slimming down will decrease the chances of a recurrence.

Chronic renal failure

Inside your cat's kidneys are thousands of tiny nephrons whose job is to filter waste matter, thus preventing it from getting into the bloodstream, and to regulate electrolytes in the cat's body. When nephrons begin to die off, as part of the life process of a cat, the kidneys start to shut down and chronic renal failure can result. The disease most often affects cats older than 7 years old, but should symptoms be present in younger cats, they should be tested immediately. It is believed that only 30 percent of a cat's kidney is needed for normal functioning, which suggests that he or she could have up to a 70 percent loss due to renal failure before any signs or symptoms present themselves. Because chronic renal failure shares symptoms with others diseases, a clinical test must be conducted by your cat's veterinarian.

Early signs of the disease include an increased thirst, as your cat tries instinctively to get more water into his or her system to move the electrolytes throughout the body, which is then followed by an increase in urination. Should the condition persist, your cat may show signs that mimic malnutrition. Appetite will decrease due to feeling nauseous. He or she may suffer from vomiting and weight loss. He or she will look emaciated and the coat will be thin and feel coarse. There are a whole host of other symptoms including licking of his lips, eating kitty litter, oral ulcerations, an ammonia-type smell to his breath, convulsions, and — if his or her condition is completely neglected — even death.

The exact cause of chronic renal failure is unknown. However, it is generally accepted that diet plays an important role in its cause and maybe even its progression. In particular, diets that are too acidified or that are deficient in potassium seem to be implicated. As just discussed, a cat must have an acidic diet, but you must not let it get too acidic, that is, his pH level must not go below 6.0. Giving your cat enough plant matter will supply enough alkalinity to maintain good health. A diet that is too acidic can lead to metabolic acidosis, where the excess acids cause toxins to build up in a cat's blood. A diet can become overly acidic if it is excessively high in meat protein without the 5 to 10 percent of carbohydrates. An extremely acidic diet will also prevent a cat from properly absorbing potassium from his foods. A lack of potassium may lead to a condition called hypokalemia, where he suffers from muscle weakness and fatigue. Together, the highly acidic environment and deficient potassium can create chronic renal failure.

Unfortunately, there currently is no cure for chronic renal failure. Your veterinarian will advise you on the proper protocol for your cat. Often veterinarians will suggest a low-salt and low-phosphorous diet for a cat suffering from chronic renal failure. Such a diet will limit the amount of waste by-products the kidneys would have to filter out.

If your cat's veterinarian does suggest altering his or her diet to address chronic renal failure, one of the first foods recommended be taken away from your cat is beef. Interestingly, cats in the wild do not regularly consume beef, even the big cats of Africa and Asia. The reason why the veterinarian will want to eliminate beef is because beef is high in the mineral phosphorous. Phosphorous will encourage the progression of the disease because cats with chronic renal failure are unable to process phosphorus correctly. Instead their bodies retain the mineral, which will lead to a condition called hyperphosphatemia, which in turn encourages yet another condition called renal secondary hyperparathyroidism. Therefore, you will want to feed your cat suffering from chronic renal failure proteins from chicken, turkey, and even egg. All proteins should be the highest quality you can find, as they produce the least amount of protein waste for the kidneys to process. Small amounts of celery might also be a good food to feed your cat with chronic renal failure, as it has a mild diuretic effect, which helps flush the system.

Inflammatory bowel disease

Humans who suffer from inflammatory bowel disease are not alone. Their cats can also develop the condition, in which inflammatory cells invade their stomach or intestines. Inflammatory cells are naturally produced in the body and play integral roles in keeping cats healthy. However, when they infiltrate the stomach or intestine of a cat, they can encourage the body to respond with inflammation as if it sensed an injury or illness.

Several different types of inflammatory cells can create inflammatory bowel disease in your cat:

- The first kind is the lymphocyte. It is a cell that works with the cat's immune system. It is the most common instigator of inflammatory bowel symptoms.

- The second kind comprises the eosinophils cells. There are a couple of different kinds of eosinophils cells, and they tend to create more severe symptoms in your cat than lymphocyte cells. In fact, eosinophils cells can create a condition in cats that is similar to the human Crohn's disease.

- A third type of inflammatory cell is the neutrophil cell. In the healthy body, this inflammatory cell is responsible for destroying bacteria or eliminating damaged tissue.

Because there are more than one kind of inflammatory bowel disease trigger cells and more than one part of the gastrointestinal tract, there are a variety of signs and symptoms of the disease. However, the two most common symptoms include diarrhea and vomiting. With some cats, owners will see an increase in the frequency of their bowel movements, but smaller stools. Sometimes mucus or blood will also be present in the stools.

As with other health conditions, the symptoms can be shared among a diversity of diseases, so always check with your cat's veterinarian for the correct diagnosis. Should your cat be diagnosed with inflammatory bowel disease, your veterinarian may suggest changing her diet. Exactly which changes will need to be made is determined by his or her particular symptoms. You may need to begin by determining if your cat has particular food sensitivities or allergies, in which case you would put him or her on a restricted diet of only one protein and one carbohydrate source for a couple of weeks. The most non-allergenic foods are lamb and rice; a diet comprised of those two ingredients — and calcium and taurine supplements as well as a multivitamin — for a couple of weeks should clear up any allergy symptoms. Once your cat is adjusted to that diet, you can slowly introduce new foods — one at a time — to see if any particular ones trigger the inflammation reaction.

A cat suffering from constipation due to inflammatory bowel disease will often improve using insoluble fiber foods as part of the carbohydrate portion of meals. Insoluble fiber is a gastrointestinal tract stimulant, which means it will encourage bowel movement. Foods containing insoluble fiber include kale, collard greens and other greens, pumpkin seeds, broccoli, and celery. As with humans, it can be very uncomfortable to eat foods containing insoluble fiber all by themselves on an empty stomach as gas pains and discomfort from constipation may result. Be sure you mix it in with meat at a regular mealtime.

At the other end of the spectrum from constipation are cats that have diarrhea as a main symptom of inflammatory bowel disease. Those cats generally do better with soluble fiber. Soluble fiber is found in the starchier carbohydrates. It is usually associated with smoother, less stringy foods than insoluble fiber. Good sources of soluble fiber for your cat include rice, oatmeal, potatoes, carrots, sweet potatoes, parsnips, squash, and pumpkins.

There are a few other dietary tidbits to keep in mind when preparing meals for a cat suffering from inflammatory bowel disease. Remember grains are very irritating to a cat's digestive tract. They will only exacerbate inflammatory bowel symptoms. You should also try to offer only one protein source at a time for easier digestion. And do not forget that when feeding your kitty any form of fiber, he or she needs to have plenty of moisture to go along with food. Even if the food seems moist to you, it might be a good idea for him or her to have a bowl of water next to the food bowl just in case your cat needs more. Also, ask your cat's veterinarian about supplements. Adding L-glutamine, probiotics, and digestive enzymes to the diet may help improve the ability to absorb nutrients.

Liver disease

A cat's liver, like all animal livers, wears many hats. A properly functioning liver removes toxins from the blood, aids in the digestion of food and the absorption of fat, converts sugars, provides the bile necessary for the fat soluble vitamins to be absorbed by the body, produces blood clotting agents, creates hormones, and helps bind ammonia so your cat can excrete it in her urine. That is a big job. But, to accomplish it all, a cat's liver is its largest internal organ.

Perhaps due to its multifunctional nature, the cat's liver is relatively sensitive and prone to particular health disorders. Cholangitis is an inflammatory condition that affects the bile duct. Hepatic lipidosis, also known as fatty liver disease, occurs when the liver builds up an excess of fat. The liver can also suffer from damage from storing too many toxins. Portosystemic shunts happen when the cat's blood bypasses the liver; therefore, it does not get detoxified. A cat can also suffer from a variety of tumors and cancers of the liver as well.

Symptoms of liver disease can vary according to the specific illness, but there are several that seem to be common among many diseases. The most easily recognized symptom is jaundice, which shows up as a yellowing of the eyes and skin. Cats with liver disease will also suffer from a loss of appetite, weight loss, lethargy, diarrhea, and vomiting. Some may have an increased thirst, possibly as an attempt to force electrolytes through the body, followed by an increase in urination. Some will even suffer from seizures and convulsions.

Only your cat's veterinarian can confirm the exact liver disease your cat is suffering. Regardless of which disease, though, there are nutritional approaches you can take to help alleviate the condition. For hepatic lipidosis, or fatty liver disease, it is imperative your cat eats a high-quality diet. Of paramount importance is the essential amino acid, taurine, found in the liver meat or in supplement form. Sometimes protein restriction may be recommended, as in a cat suffering with a portosystemic shunt, a condition discussed above. With most liver problems, cats benefit from eating frequent, small meals of the best organic products you can find. Non-organic foodstuffs can have toxins in them that will only increase the stress on your cat's liver to function.

Cancer

Often, humans are shocked to learn that their beloved felines can get cancer. Many individuals seem to think cancer is a human condition but sadly, it is not. In fact, cats suffer from cancer at a higher rate than humans. Skin cancer is most prevalent and is responsible for about 25 percent of all cat cancers. Inside the body, the feline leukemia virus is the cause of nearly half of all internal cancers.

Cancer happens when, instead of healthy body functions occurring, cells rapidly divide and grow tissue. The tissue is what forms a tumor. The body organs near the tumor formation suffer from the non-regeneration of healthy cells because the body is focused on reproducing the malignant cells. Those organs slowly die off while the tumor grows.

Only your cat's veterinarian can determine whether or not your cat has cancer and which kind. The vet will then counsel you on which course of action would be best for your beloved pet. Many of the treatment modalities offered to humans are also available to your cat — surgery, chemotherapy, and radiation. Your vet may also make recommendations for both conventional and alternative therapies. And he or she will want to discuss your cat's diet and nutrition, as nutrition is playing an increasingly prevalent role in cancer therapy for cats.

Cats and cancer facts

About 32 percent of all cats over the age of 10 will die from cancer; a few of the most prevalent cat cancers include the following:

- **Brain cancer:** A cancer of the brain or spinal canal. Because brain cancer can progress for a long time before symptoms to show up, it usually affects older cats more than kittens and younger cats.

- **Mammary carcinoma:** Better known as breast cancer and concerns female cats, particularly ones that were never spayed or that were spayed at an older age.

- **Mastocytoma:** A tumor created by mast cells in the body, creates severe allergic reactions, affects about 20 percent of cat cancers

- **Squamous cell carcinoma:** A form of cancer that most commonly affects the mouth, toenails, tonsils, and tongue in cats.

- **Hemangiosarcoma:** A type of cancer where blood vessels grow directly into the tumor, but is more common in canines than felines.

- **Lymphoma:** Blood cancer; cats are five times more susceptible to it than humans.

- **Melanoma:** A dangerous type of skin cancer, more of a concern for cats that have darker skin pigmentation.

- **Osteosarcoma:** An aggressive bone cancer.

- **Testicular cancer:** Cancer of the testicles, affects male cats that have not been neutered.

If your cat is diagnosed with cancer, a key concept to remember when feeding him or her is that it seems like cancerous cells love carbohydrates, but do not feel the same about fat and protein. Many veterinarians suggest restricting carbohydrates to no more than 5 percent of a cat's diet, and ensuring those carbohydrates are of both soluble and insoluble fiber. A mixture of peas, pumpkin, rice, and psyllium will be most beneficial because it is high in antioxidants, easy to digest, and pleasing to his or her taste buds. You should eliminate all simple carbohydrates, including any prepackaged treats, milk, and kibble because they will fill your cat up without giving him or her the beneficial fiber and antioxidants. Adding fish oils, which are heavy with omega-3 fatty acids, to a cat's diet is an integral part of cancer therapy, as the fat will not feed the cancer. Digestive enzymes should be added to the meal as well, because they may help with the absorption of essential nutrients. The amino acid, arginine, is also being considered as a nutritional therapy, although its exact role is still being investigated.

A side problem of cats suffering from cancer is a decreased appetite. Unfortunately, if you allow your cat to stop eating, quality of life will decrease, response to treatment will suffer, and survival may be shortened. There are plenty of tips to encourage eating at the end of this chapter. If you have tried the tips and your cat still refuses to eat after a couple of days, seek help from your veterinarian. Another underlying condition may need to be addressed.

Heart problems

Like cancer, most pet owners are aware of the potential for humans to be diagnosed with heart disease, but few probably realize that their cats can be diagnosed with the deadly condition as well. The truth of the matter is, the heart of a cat is probably its hardest working muscle. In fact, though a feline body is much smaller than its human owner, the cat's heart beats twice as fast as the humans. Cats can either inherit the tendency to get the disease or they can acquire it later in life. Inheritance does not suggest that it is only effects particular breeds. Interestingly, all cat breeds have the potential to be born with the problem, but particular breeds seem more prone to acquire specific forms of it later in life.

Regardless of whether or not a cat is born with a congenital or inherited form of heart disease, or if she acquires it, the symptoms are often the same; the most common signs are a decreased tolerance for movement and exercise, weakness, and coughing. Other symptoms include a lack of appetite, an extended stomach, a bluish tint to the gums, tongue and lips, and even the tendency to fall unconscious. One of the unfortunate aspects of all feline heart disease is that often, by the time the cat shows symptoms, the condition is already fairly advanced. It is possible, though, that by sheer coincidence a veterinarian will pick up on a heart murmur during a regular check up, before the onset of any symptoms of the disease.

Hereditary heart disease: The three most common inherited, or congenital, heart diseases include mitral valve malformation, tricuspid valve malformation, and ventricular septal defects. As their names suggest, the first two occur when specific heart valves are malformed, and the last happens when there is an abnormality on the septum that separates the right and left heart ventricles. If a cat is suffering from a hereditary heart disease, he or she will usually show symptoms, and even suffer from heart failure while still a kitten before she is ten months old.

Acquired heart disease: Also called cardiomyopathy, acquired heart disease is a weakening of the heart or a shift in the structure of the heart muscles. Similar to the congenital problems, there are three main forms of cardiomyopathy. The different varieties are determined by how exactly the heart walls are affected.

- **Hypertrophic cardiomyopathy:** The most common form that is seen in adult cats, hypertrophic cardiomyopathy is the most successfully treated form. It occurs when the areas of the heart enlarge, thicken, and become stiff so the left ventricle decreases in size and becomes unable to fill and pump blood to the other organs. This condition can result in congestive heart failure. The exact cause of this type of cardiomyopathy is unknown. What is known, however, is that particular breeds seem to be more prone to developing hypertrophic cardiomyopathy. It is most often seen in the American Shorthairs, Maine Coons, Persian, and Ragdoll breeds.

- **Dilated cardiomyopathy:** Dilated cardiomyopathy occurs when the heart muscles weaken and cause the chambers to grow larger. Thankfully, veterinarians are diagnosing dilated cardiomyopothy with less and less frequency. It was determined that a lack of the essential amino acid taurine was the primary cause. Pet food manufacturers now regularly add taurine to their cat products to help prevent the disease.

- **Restrictive cardiomyopathy:** The rarest form of heart disease in cats is restrictive cardiomyopathy. It is seen most frequently in senior cats. It occurs when the heart weakens to the point where it cannot pump blood effectively. The blood then pools in the atrium, causing it to expand. This particular cardiomyopathy is the most difficult for a veterinarian to detect, as it is not easily found on an echocardiogram — the primary tool for examining hearts.

To confirm the diagnosis of heart disease, your cat's veterinarian may want to have X-rays and electrocardiograms taken, Doppler imaging conducted, and have blood work drawn. Should your cat be diagnosed with a heart disease, treatment will depend on how advanced it is. Currently, there is no cure for the condition, so the goal will be to manage it and keep your cat as healthy and comfortable as you can. Most often, a prescription medication will be suggested along with changes to his diet and activity.

As for medication, some veterinarians will prescribe similar pharmaceutical products that human doctors suggest for their patients to reduce and prevent the buildup of fluid in the chest area — beta-blockers, diuretics, and vasodilators. Beta-blockers help slow nerve impulses as they travel through the heart. Diuretics help the body get rid of excess retained water, which helps the heart pump and control blood pressure. Additionally, vasodilators make the walls of the blood vessels relax and widen so that blood flows more easily. Holistic veterinarians will frequently turn toward herbs and other natural remedies with a tradition of heart healing. Hawthorn, or *Crataegus oxycantha,* has performed well in controlled, clinical studies and contains antioxidants that support and strengthen arteries. The homeopathic remedies Arnica montana, Calcium fluoride, and Kalium phosphate are also used to help maintain blood pressure.

If your cat is suffering from any of these aliments, your veterinarian will advise you about your cat's needs. Most will tell you to keep salt at a minimum and increase taurine intake. You may need to provide additional taurine in supplement form to your cat as well as a coenzyme Q10 antioxidant supplement, which tones and strengthens the heart. Many holistic veterinarians will even encourage you to switch your cat to a raw foods diet; while you will need to continue to be sure your cat continues eating high-protein meals, celery is often suggested for cats suffering from heart disease. Celery has phthalide in it; an active compound that will relax arterial muscles. It is also a mild diuretic, and it will help reduce the buildup of fluid in the heart area.

Miscellaneous needs

You can administer a variety of herbs and natural remedies to your cat for less serious conditions than those listed above. Though many cat owners have used the following suggestions, they may not be right for your cat. If you believe any of them might be a good fit for your tabby, discuss it with your veterinarian before you proceed. Cats are just like their human owners — each one is unique. What works to relieve an ailment for one cat may not work for the same condition in another.

Stress

Some cats are easily stressed while others do not seem to be affected by major catastrophes. If there are particular uncontrollable, yet predictable events, such as thunderstorms or a home relocation, there are a few options available to help soothe your tom. Many owners have had great success with flower essences; a few drops in the mouth will ease many a jittery cat. Catnip, either brewed into a tea and poured over food, or given directly as a treat will also help cats mellow out. Though catnip may make some cats excitable, so be sure you know what to expect prior to offering it to your nervous tom.

Arthritis and joint pain

Cats are not immune to the joint swelling and tenderness known as arthritis. Glucosamine, which is often used to treat human arthritis, can be effective in alleviating the symptoms of the disorder. Ointments containing calendula, red alder, and neem oil, all of which can be found in your local natural health or herbal supplement store, can also be rubbed onto a tabby that does not mind the slight smell and sensation of it on his or her hair. Be cautious when applying any kind of ointment, though, as many cats will react as if it were dirt or another factor soiling his or her beautiful fur, and they may do their best to groom it off.

Ear mites

Occasionally, even in the best-groomed cats, microscopic parasites will find their way into the cat's ear canal. These critters, called ear mites, are highly contagious, and your cat can share them with other animals in the household, including dogs and rabbits, but not humans. If your cat is scratching incessantly at her ears or shaking her head non-stop, she may have ear mites. If there is an infestation, the inside of the ears will appear to be dirty as if reddish-brown or black tiny grains of sand are stuck to the ear. If your veterinarian diagnoses your cat with ear mites, you will need to clean out your tom's ears with warm, soapy water. Be careful, because your cat may not enjoy this particular form of affection from you. You may want to find a helper to restrain and comfort your cat as much as possible during the cleaning. You might even consider one of the stress relievers mentioned above. Applying natural oils of garlic, mullein, neem, and olive, or a combination of all of them, may help prevent infections that can arise from ear mite infestation.

Skin irritation

Cats are renowned for their beautiful coats, but they are not exempt from suffering from either episodic or chronic skin conditions. Stress, changing weather conditions, illnesses, pest infestations, and nutrition deficiencies can affect the health and look of their skin. Excessive shedding or paw licking, dull coats that were once shiny, greasy coats that were once matte, eczema, and dermatitis can be helped by increasing omega-3 and omega-6 fatty acids in your cat's diet. Omega-3 is most commonly found in cold-water fish, and omega-6 fatty acids are more commonly found in beef. Both are easily available in supplement form where the omega-6 is derived from borage oil. Some cat owners have also found burdock, poured in tea form over dry kibble, helps improve the skin's condition.

Upset stomach

As you make changes to your cat's diet, he or she may suffer an occasional upset stomach or intestinal distress. Look for the stomach appearing more distended than usual, gas, and grumbling noises coming from the insides. Your cat also may be irritable and not want to be touched or disturbed. In such cases, caraway and dill sprinkled on food, or poured over it in tea form can offer relief.

Ringworm

Contrary to its name, ringworm is not a worm. It is actually a fungal infection. If you find a bald spot on your cat's skin, take him or her immediately to your veterinarian. Ringworm is highly contagious, and you and your other human family members can get it from your cat. Your veterinarian will probably suggest an antifungal treatment as well as an internal medicine. A more natural way to deal with ringworm is to apply highly concentrated colloidal silver — found in your local health food store's supplement section — to the area six times a day. The bottle of colloidal silver will tell you how many parts per million are in the bottle, that is how many milligrams of silver are deposited into 1 liter of water (which equals one million particles of silver) to create the product. For ringworm, you will want to find a product that is at least 150 ppm, but you can go as high as 500 ppm if you can find it. As with anything having to do with your cat, be sure to discuss this option with your veterinarian. Regardless of the technique, it is also imperative that you thoroughly wash, with soap and a diluted bleach solution, your cat's bedding and any areas in the house that he or she frequents, as any ringworm fungal spores found there can reinfect your cat.

Bee stings

Cats love to run after butterflies, birds, and anything else that looks like it would make for a delightful mid-afternoon hunt. However, "anything else" also includes bees, and the occasional sting ensues. If you find your tom received the business end of a bee, gently wash the area with warm water before trying to alleviate the pain. The homeopathic remedy Apis can be given orally in medicine form if he or she is acting like the sting is aggravating. Other natural remedies for bee stings include mixing a paste of baking soda and water and applying it to the site or dropping organic apple cider vinegar onto the sting from a soaked cotton swab. Neither method is toxic to your cat if used in the quantity necessary for a small amount over a bee sting. However, if your kitty decides to groom the baking soda off and develops a strong liking for the taste of baking soda, he would be a rare cat indeed, but you should refrain from letting him or her have it to eat. Ingesting large, measuring-cup-sized amounts of the baking soda could cause a dangerous electrolyte imbalance and lead to heart problems.

Most of the time bee stings are minor nuisances for your cat, but just as with humans, sometimes they tolerate the first sting just fine only to become allergic to it and have a major issue the next time they are stung. So, keep a close eye on your tom if he is stung a second time. Also, if the sting happens inside the mouth, you will want to take him or her to a veterinarian immediately. Should any inflammation result due to the sting, it could potentially block airways and cause suffocation.

Cat scratches

Whether they mean to because they are in a bad mood, or if it just happens by accident during rough play, many cats scratch the other cat members of the household. If your tabby appears to have a superficial wound inflicted by one of the housemates, it is imperative you clean it. Cat claws can easily pick up bacteria from the litter box and transplant it into a flesh wound where it can fester. First, wash the area with soapy water, (and know full well that he or she will hate you for it). Once clean, you can apply stevia extract — if you do not have the liquid, use the powder mixed with water. Stevia will help stop the bleeding and encourage healing. Even better than mixing the stevia with water, mix it with colloidal silver, for an antibacterial treatment. Of course, if the wound cannot be labeled superficial and looks deeper, get your cat to her veterinarian as soon as possible.

Cat scratch fever

It is not just a risqué song by Ted Nugent, but it is an actual illness caused by a cat scratch. When kitties use a litter box, they tend to scratch the litter over the waste. Because of that tidy habit, a bacterium from the wastes gets lodged into the nails. Should a human be scratched with the nail, that bacteria can get planted into the skin and cause an infection needing medical care.

Tips for Getting Your Cat to Eat

While not a physical ailment or health condition, a cat refusing to eat can be a cause for concern. Sometimes it is just difficult to get your cat to eat. In particular, cats recovering from surgery, illness, dealing with stress, or other medical trauma will refuse to eat even their favorite foods. Equally, some cats may revolt at any changes to their diet regardless of how good their human owners think it smells. They will turn their noses up at their personal serving dish and walk away. Patience, a willingness to experiment with techniques and ideas, and a sense of humor are generally necessary during those trying times.

You can also try warming the food in a microwave for just a few seconds. This idea works especially well with kittens that seem to prefer foods that are warm like a mother's milk, but it may also be a good idea to try warming food with older cats. Heating it up will increase the aroma of the food and make it more appetizing to your tabby because it is believed cats will not eat what they cannot smell. However, you must remain cautious of your microwave. Microwaves do not heat in a uniform manner. Colder areas may surround warmer, even scalding "hot pockets" of food. Your unsuspecting cat risks burning the inside of his or her mouth if nibbling on cold foods and suddenly biting into a hot area. Stirring the food before serving it will help distribute and mix the hot and cold areas evenly.

If your cat tends to balk at non-meat food items, you can try to make them more palatable to her with cat condiments. Real bacon bits, dried fish flakes, pureed livers, and clam, tuna, or salmon juice can all be poured over the non-meat foods to entice your cat. You can also try pouring chicken or beef broth over the non-protein foods, combining them thoroughly together. If you are using a commercial broth, however, read the ingredients to be sure there is no onion or other potentially toxic ingredient.

If your cat continues to snub the lower-protein or carbohydrate foods, you will need to go undercover with them. An easy way to camouflage the unwanted foods is to mix them in a plastic bag with the oil or water retained from a can of tuna, anchovies, or sardines and store, sealed, in the refrigerator overnight. The fish aroma will mask the other foods. The next time you try this technique, use a smaller amount of water or oil. Continue decreasing the fish products with each batch you create until your cat eats the non-protein foods without the fish amendments.

If your feline enjoys company when eating, you can try to coax him or her into trying a new food. In an area that is away from the bowl, sit your cat on your lap, stroke him or her, and talk to him or her. When your cat is calm and relaxed, offer a tasty tidbit directly from your hand. Allow your cat to sniff at it and poke it with his or her nose. Your cat may or may not eat it the first time, but if he or she refuses without jumping off your lap try again the next day. Eventually, your cat will nibble, and at that point, you can place some in his or her dish.

Remember, liquid is very important in your cat's diet; instinctively, your cat knows this. However, your cat also has particular tastes and enjoys watching confused humans try to figure out how to please him or her. If you notice your cat is not drinking the water in the dish, but is not against jumping up onto the sink counter to drink from the tap, he or she may prefer running water, the way ancestors drank from rivers. Some owners are able to simulate the running water phenomenon by placing a small, tabletop water fountain next to the cat's food dish *(see Resources for shopping suggestions)* where the cat can drink from moving water at his or her leisure. Not only will it encourage your cat to drink the water, but also it will also provide a Zen-like peaceful feeling in the dining environment.

Finally, if you know catnip will not make your cat go to sleep, you can try mixing a small amount with meals. Though humans cannot smell it, there is a chemical in catnip called nepetalactone, for which some cats have a special receptor in their olfactory system not completely understood yet by veterinary scientists. What is known is that kittens and senior cats seem to be immune to catnip, and there seems to be a genetic predisposition as to whether or not an adult will respond to it. In essence, only about 66 percent of cats respond to it, so this technique will not work for all cats. For non-senior adult cats — cats around 12 years old and younger — though, try it with full awareness that it may make your tom overly protective of his food. Your cat may even attempt to growl if someone approaches the food dish when there is catnip in it, as he may not want anyone else near his favorite herb.

Regardless of the age or stage of life of your cat, proper nourishment will help prevent a host of health conditions, alleviate symptoms, and even assist in the treatment of many common diseases and illnesses. Good quality whole foods are only the beginning of natural cat care, though. Once you feel comfortable with the changes in diet, you may want to expand the natural or holistic reach of your efforts into the rest of his or her environment.

CHAPTER
8

Being the Personal Chef to a Cat

· · · · · · · · · · · · · · · · · · · ·

Now that you know the basic requirements for creating nutritional meals to feed your cat, you may think you are ready to head into the kitchen and start chopping, grinding, and mixing meat and vegetables for your kitty. However, before you start, there are a few more things to consider and prepare you for your new lifestyle as personal chef.

Changing Mind-sets

You must be prepared for family and close friends to be less supportive than you would like them to be as you go through the process of converting your cat's diet from the "normal" one of commercial food to a natural, home-prepared one. As with every new change in your life, there will be a learning curve as you rearrange your time and even storage space in the refrigerator. If you have a home filled with people not used to those new activities, you may find some resistance and maybe even a little resentment because your focus is temporarily redirected. The key word here is temporarily. You may need to remind everyone of the benefits and that once the process is complete, all will be back to normal again.

It might also be necessary to keep reminding everyone of the benefits your cat will get from the diet change. Your family may be excited about the potential for the family's older cat becoming healthy and kitten-like again, but teenagers may grimace at plopping a couple of tablespoons of ground up rabbit into the cat's dish. Likewise, spouses or significant others who are not used to cooking or handling meats, may not realize they have issues with it as well. Getting and keeping everyone focused on the long-term benefits might help them all get over the "ick-factor" of the moment.

Other new behaviors will also have to be encouraged and enforced. For example, you will no longer be able to fill your tom's dish in the morning and leave it out all day. You will be putting out unprocessed food, which means there will be the potential for bacteria to grow in the food left out for hours at room temperature. The food can oxidize and even grow rancid if left unattended long enough. Fresh meats may also tempt ants and other unwanted critters from outside if the food is left uncovered out in the open. Whoever is in charge of feeding the cat that day must remember — and be willing — to clean the bowls after the kitty dines.

Peer pressure

A quick Internet search will provide literally hundreds, if not thousands, of testimonials and anecdotal proof of the power and wonder of creating and serving your cat an all-natural diet. You may find after a few months of doing it for your fabulous feline that you are inspired to follow suit and provide your own story for the world to read about. It would be a great idea if you do, as the more people learn about the potential negatives of feeding low-quality commercial foods to their pets, the more they will want to improve the diet of their own animals. Your story will only help the groundswell movement that, possibly, will help all pets everywhere.

But you need to be aware that feeding your cat an all-natural diet, even one where you find miraculous results, is not without its downside. Many cat owners feel as though they are being scrutinized under a negative microscope when they mention to anyone they feed their cats an all-natural or raw-food diet. As Cat Writer Association member Robin Olson put it, "feeding raw is like being part of an underground cult." Cat owners who have personally experienced the sometimes jaw-dropping positive results of a natural foods diet for cats quickly learn they may not always feel comfortable discussing what they are doing behind closed kitchen doors. After receiving the disparaging remarks and disapproving looks from their veterinarians, it is sometimes difficult to talk about the decision with earnest frankness. And yet, it is so tempting: When you see a friend or neighbor's cat suffer like yours once did, you want to offer help and assistance. However, when that friend asks: "Really? It worked for you? What did your vet say about it?" And you answer: "He said it was a bad idea for cats to eat human food." You feel as if you lose all credibility.

Feeling comfortable discussing feeding your cats homemade food is made even more difficult if you made the switch as a preemptive measure before your cat developed a health issue. Because then you cannot even say: "Look! See how much better she is now?" If you find yourself feeling defensive when you talk about it or opting not to mention anything about it, you may begin to question your own motives. Do as much research as you can to help ease any discomfort. Building a solid research foundation to support your personal experience and load up on anecdotal proof to help give you the confidence to counter the "What does your vet think?" question. As you further educate yourself, you will be able to educate the cat lovers around you. Then your cat will become a living example of how healthy a raw or natural foods diet can be.

Finding support

No matter where you are in the process of feeding your cat a natural foods diet — either at the thinking stage or the completely onboard stage — there are plenty of opportunities to find external support and maybe even further your impact. Once you get your footing and feel strong enough to discuss it with family, friends, and coworkers, seek out other cat owners in your area. There are plenty of local cat groups across the country; do your research, and find some who are close to you. Ask fellow cat owners, or do an Internet search for "cat club," and see what comes up. Another idea is to check with your local animal shelters. They may be in contact with pet owners housing temporary foster cats. People who are that involved will be knowledgeable regarding potential cat clubs or groups. You can also check the bulletin boards in pet stores and even in health-food stores, because — really — where else will raw or natural food proponents be buying their food?

If there is not a club in your area, you can start one. You can recruit members from some of the resources mentioned above, or you can become a local expert. Contact your area parks and recreation department and see if you can offer a class or public speaking engagement concerning cat nutrition. Check out the organizations that meet at the nearby library branches to see if there is one related to animals where you can go and discuss your experience feeding your cat a natural diet. Also, if you find a veterinarian who supports your decision, ask if you can leave flyers out in his office to encourage interested cat owners to join you.

Once you get a groundswell of people supporting you, start looking to network with other groups in your geographical area. There really is power in the people. Eventually, raw and natural food proponents will be found all around the country. The more people become aware of the necessity for feeding cats raw or natural foods, the more power there will be to make it happen easily. More suppliers will appear on the market, and pet food stores will have to buy their products. Maybe even traditional pet food manufacturers will try to create their own lines of frozen meats, instead of kibble of unknown origin.

Whom to contact

The Internet will be a valuable resource to find people willing to become an organized group of cat health advocates. If there are no veterinarians in your immediate area, you will be able to locate them via your favorite search engine, such as Google (**www.google.com**) or Bing™ (**www.bing.com**). Getting professionals such as veterinarians on board with your organization will make your voice louder and help — possibly — convert the traditional vets.

Your local animal shelter may also be a good resource for you to contact. A few animal shelters do feed raw and natural diets to their animals, but the majority do not. Many of these smaller shelters house too many animals, have a small kitchen — if any — and rely on donations. Others, such as the Dharma Rescue group, rely on foster families who follow their strict diet regimens. You will find most of them only feed their animals commercial foods. Often, it is donated commercial food that they do not purchase for themselves; therefore, they cannot say: "No, thank you." The people who work at these smaller shelters have big animal-loving hearts, and they would be more than happy to hear about raw and natural cat food stories. They would also be willing to tell adoptive owners about your cats, and probably — if you have flyers or business cards available — they will help recruit for your cause.

CASE STUDY: A NATURAL PET SHELTER ORGANIZATION

Susan Fulcher

Dharma Rescue for Cats and Dogs and Dharma Rescue for Cats and Dogs Store

24325 Crenshaw Blvd.

Torrance, California 90505

Adoption: 310-326-8881

Store: 310-326-8881

www.dharmarescue.org

The Dharma Rescue group started out as a grooming pet store, selling dry and canned pet food. The food they carried was natural, processed food. The owners knew people on the raw food diet but, like most, were fearful of salmonella and other dangerous bacteria. At the time, the owner, Susan Fulcher, had a very sick boxer named Mona. Genetics, over vaccinating, and a processed diet caused her to develop a life-threatening autoimmune disease. Her path in life at the time had her questioning what she was feeding her animals, and she started to turn to a more natural and spiritual way, which introduced her to a holistic vet named Dr. Dee Blanco, who gave Fulcher the guidance to naturally care for her animals. One of the first things she asked Fulcher to do was feed Mona a raw diet. Through homeopathy, diet, and supplements, she saved the dog's life and helped her live a quality life until she passed at 12 years of age.

After seeing the amazing transformation in this dog and the new vital force she gained, Fulcher started feeding all her animals a raw food diet. The first cat adopted to live at the store was a 6-month-old rescue kitten she named Lily. A conventional vet thought they should get rid of her because she was so sick, but Dr. Dee told her to feed the kitten raw. Within two months, this kitten was well. She has never been sick throughout the 10 years of her life.

They started rescuing more dogs and cats during the next 12 years and had changed the store into a 100 percent raw food store, without any dry or can foods being sold. Soon, all the rescued animals they collected there were thriving on a raw diet. Their health improved, and they had better temperaments.

After rescuing for many years and the store supporting the feeding of these animals, Fulcher decided to give the store over to the rescue outfit after it became a 501(c)(3) non-profit corporation (a designation meaning that the business group has been approved by the Internal Revenue Service as a tax-exempt, charitable organization). The store continues to struggle to afford to feed all the rescues, which are mostly cats. They still need to count on donations for food and vet bills. Even though it is an ongoing struggle to feed raw, they refuse to go back to processed food. The organization weighed the difference many times at board meetings, and they could not decide to deny feeding raw because they had fewer vet bills and, with the smaller cats, they had less smelly stools and better coats that did not mat. Aggressive cats became calmer, and they all lived in harmony in the cattery. "The transformation was amazing," said Fulcher.

One downfall of feeding raw is that it takes longer for the Dharma Rescue group to place their cats and kittens into adoptive homes. Their biggest fear is if the adoptive home decides to not continue with raw, the cat will revert back to the way it came to the shelter — poor coat, smelly stool, more hair balls, and viruses popping up from stress.

All of the animals they adopt are to be returned if the adoptive home does not want them. "We really try to prevent that by — first — asking on the application if the home is willing to feed raw," said Fulcher. "If they say yes and the adoption is approved, we educate them on feeding raw." There is information on their website (**www.dharmarescue.org**), and they send the families home with food to get started. Adoptive families can also find stores in the area of the adoptive homes that have raw food. These stores are always available to the adoptive homes if they need any support. Fulcher said, "Sometimes Dharma Rescue will even set up with our holistic vet an educational consult, but that is only if funds are available to pay for the consult."

The Dharma Rescue group is very strict with their kitten adoption because when they get kittens, they are started on raw food and are raised naturally. They have never had dry or canned food, are not vaccinated, and get spayed and neutered when they are a little older. Because of this natural rearing protocol, their kittens are special. They have beautiful coats and great dispositions. Anyone that has been fortunate enough to adopt one of their naturally reared cats has been very pleased.

"Dharma is a holistic rescue group, and our open-mined conventional vet first examines any animal that comes to them," Fulcher said. "If there are health issues we consult with our holistic vet. The conventional and holistic vet work together to heal all the rescues. Dharma takes in handicapped, sick, and senior animals. They never give up on the sick ones. They have taken in cats with diabetes, IBD, kidney failure, liver disease, upper respiratory, and so many other diseases. The most important factor in their healing is the diet."

You, as Head Chef

Cooking for your cat should be a labor of love. The time and energy you put into preparing a healthy, natural diet for your furry friend will have positive consequences to last throughout his or her lifetime. It may seem overwhelming at first, but as you get into the groove of it and practice it long enough to start seeing the results, you will find it to be an enjoyable pastime. You will eventually discover your own shortcuts and time management strategies to streamline the process, so that it is easily assimilated into the rest of your life.

Your cat, on the other hand, will suddenly realize the kitchen is his or her favorite room in the house. As head chef, you will need to take precautions lest your tabby gets into trouble. Once your cat realizes just how delicious your foods are, he or she may imitate your neighbor's Doberman pincer and take a sudden interest in the garbage. You must make sure that your trash can and all of your storage containers with foodstuffs in them are completely closed and airtight. You know first-hand the beautiful acrobatic acts your cat can do once he or she decides to do them. Should your cat decide to sniff around the trash can, he or she is perfectly capable of making it happen.

You must also keep a clean kitchen. Yes, alley cats and cats in the wild eat their food covered with dirt, and they do so on dusty side streets and in grassy fields, but your cat has never had that introduction to microbes. The food dish will grow mold, and the water dish will attract mildew, if they are not cleaned on a regular basis. Hand washing is fine, but if the cat bowl is dishwasher safe, as are most ceramic, glass, and stainless steels bowls, that machine might be a better option. The heat and steam inside an automatic dishwasher will kill most harmful bacteria.

How to Shop for Your Cat's Natural Menu

One of the ways you can convince the people in your household and fellow cat owners that feeding a natural diet is the right way to go is to fill them in on how easy it is to shop for your cat. You will probably find your shopping list requires you to make fewer stops. Trips to the pet specialty store can be few and far between. Instead, you will be buying meats, vegetables, and rice at the same place you food shop for the rest of the family. You only need to go to the pet supply store if there is a particular supplement, toy, or other non-food item you would like to get for your tabby.

If you become familiar with the butchers in your grocer's meat department, you may be able to special order meats, such as rabbit, quail, and pheasant from them. They also may be happy to reserve chicken fat, livers, and hearts for you as well. Otherwise, the Internet will be your friend. There are plenty of online suppliers of raw meats *(see Resources in the Appendix)* and natural food products for your cat. And for your non-meat food items, that is, for the carbohydrate sources, you will want to purchase the same quality you feed your human members of the family.

Keeping a Food Diary

Between all the foods your cat can and cannot have and all the supplements he or she needs, but not too much of, it may seem a bit overwhelming. One way to manage your cat's diet is to keep a food diary on her and the evolution of the diet. *In the Appendix, you will find a sample, blank diary page detailing the kind of information you may want to keep on your tabby's eating habits and your culinary efforts.*

At the beginning of the process, you will find the diary instrumental for maintaining lists of what your cat liked, did not like, and how well your cat tolerated each new food. You can track how much was eaten, reaction to the food, and whether or not a little coaxing was needed to try it. You may also want to notate whether or not your cat needed more moisture to go with the food. And of course, notate if there was any sort of tummy troubles or allergic reactions.

As you move along with the change and fully convert your cat over to all-natural foods, you will continue to find the diary indispensable. You can note the date of making large batches of foods that you have stored in the freezer and how long items have been thawed in the refrigerator. You will also need to be sure you do not keep foods for too long in the refrigerator, so you may want to track their length of stay to keep from accidentally serving your tabby spoiled food. Your diary will help keep you from falling into the trap of serving the same foods over and over again. Remember, the bigger the variety, the better the nutrition for your cat.

For some cat owners, the food diary eventually serves as a journal where they document their cat's life. They track weight gain, weight loss, veterinary check-ups, and health status. Some owners record favorite activities, special events, and even attach photographs of the cat with family members. *Again, see the Appendix for an example food diary.* Of course, all the added bells and whistles are not necessary, but regardless, tracking your cat's food intake and reaction to it will be indispensable for you as her personal chef.

Storing Food

Now that you have everyone, if not most everyone, in the family as on board as they are willing to go, you have shopped for all the necessary foodstuffs, and you have the diary at the ready to start compiling, it is time to get started preparing the food. Because the serving size for your cat is very small compared to a human's, it would be very inconvenient to prepare a meal each time you feed your cat. You will want to prepare larger meals and then freeze them in individual serving sizes.

Remember, rules for freezing foods for human consumption apply to freezing home-prepared cat foods. Those rules include the fact that you must eat the food upon thawing and before any spoiling begins. Freezing food to 0 degrees Fahrenheit will inactivate bacteria and mold in the food indefinitely, but only while it remains frozen. Once thawed, those microbes will become active again and multiply at the same rate as they do in fresh food. Also, you cannot refreeze food that had started to thaw as it is impossible to tell how far in the reactivation process of the bacteria and mold is during thawing. Therefore, refreezing foods and then re-thawing them may give you a false idea of how long you have before you need to feed the foods to your cat, and you may inadvertently give him or her food that is spoiled without knowing it.

Freezing foods in snack-sized, resealable bags is ideal for keeping serving sizes readily available for you to feed to your cat. You can label and date the bag and then thaw them in the refrigerator the day before you put the food in his or her dish. Another technique that many cat owners prefer is to freeze the prepared meals in ice cube trays. Follow the simple steps below to freeze your cat's food properly.

1. Prepare the food according to the recipe directions.

2. Scoop the food into ice cube tray sections.

3. Place the ice cube tray into a sealed plastic bag to keep the food from drying out.

4. Put the ice cube tray, within its bag, into the freezer.

5. Once frozen, empty the trays into large resealable bags, as bags will take up less space in your freezer than several ice cube trays.

6. Depending on the size of the cube compartments of your trays, you will need to thaw one or two cubes of food for each meal.

One final thing to keep in mind when freezing and serving frozen meals — freezer burn happens when food is exposed to too much air as it freezes. Foods with freezer burn will not be harmful, but they become unappetizing to both humans and cats. In particular, meats will appear to have a leathery quality, and they will feel and look dry. The flavor and texture suffers in freezer-burned foods, as well. They may even evolve to the point where your picky kitty will rebel and refuse to eat it. Only the parts that look freezer-burned will have the different taste or texture, though, so you can cut off the freezer-burned part, and the rest will be accepted by your royal feline.

Preparing raw meals

If you choose to go the raw food route, you will find a heavy-duty meat grinder to be your best friend. There are a variety of meat grinders on the market at an equally variable price range. You will need to find one strong enough to grind bones, which means you will probably need to purchase a more expensive grinder. You should expect to spend at least $100. Look for a grinder with all metal internal parts, at least two, preferably three, sizes of grinding plates, and a motor wattage over 100. Northern Tool and Equipment has a few you can order from its website (**www.northerntool.com**). The Waring Professional Electric Meat Grinder has also been successfully used for raw cat (and dog) food and can be found on the Food Network's shopping website (**www.foodnetworkstore.com**).

It is best to grind the whole animal to be sure you are getting all the nutrients from it. When you hear the words "whole animal," this means the organ and muscle meat, bone, and fat of a particular animal. If you are unable to grind the entire animal, you will need to remember to mix in calcium and taurine supplements. But if you are grinding raw bones, you will probably not need to add in calcium. As mentioned previously, cats can eat raw bones. It is only when bones are cooked that they become brittle and potentially harmful.

Grinding meats can be a messy and somewhat labor-intensive business. You will want to set aside a Saturday or Sunday afternoon to prepare several batches of ground meals for your cat that will last you a month or two. To help contain the mess, many people take plastic bags and cover the entire surface of their kitchen counters to make clean up easy. When the grinding is done, they carefully wad up the bags with the drippings and leftover bits inside to throw away. In addition to the grinder and plastic bags, you will need a large cutting board, sharp knives, several bowls, and towels. The following steps are good guidelines when you begin to grind raw meats.

1. **The first step will be to cut the meat into pieces small enough to fit into your grinder.**

   - Each machine is different, so there may be a trial-and-error period at the beginning.

   - If cutting a bird, generally you can cut it down the center, then cut at each joint, and finally, cut from side-to-side on the front and back pieces. Of course, if your grinder's opening is even smaller, you may need to cut the pieces even smaller.

   - As you feed the chunks of meat down the grinder's chute, you may want to give the machine a break periodically, especially if there are several bones, so that you do not burn out your motor.

2. **Allow all portions of the animal to mix together.**

   - You may find it convenient to position the grinder so that the ground meat falls out of the machine and directly into a large bowl or stockpot in the kitchen sink.

   - Once the meat is ground, you can add in vegetables, rice, and broth according to the recipes you choose.

   - Mix everything thoroughly together in the pot or bowl, and then spoon into the small, resealable bags or ice cube trays for freezing.

3. **Clean up.**

   - Carefully gather all the leftovers into the trash bags.

   - Afterward, you may want to spray the counters with a disinfecting spray just to be sure no bacteria are left behind.

   - You will need to wash the grinder and all the parts thoroughly, according to the manufacturer's directions.

- Some grinder parts can be washed in a dishwasher, which at high temperatures, will also disinfect them.

- The disks and other metal parts of the grinder will benefit from a light rubbing of olive oil after each use and cleaning to help prevent rusting.

There are a few things to consider when grinding meat, whether you feel as though you are a seasoned grinder, or this is your first time.

- The first couple of times you grind meat, you may want to use your grinder's disk with the smallest holes. Once your cat is accustomed to meat ground very fine, you can move up to the next size holes, and eventually to the largest setting.

- If you have a grinder that does not grind bones, you will need to be sure to supplement the calcium in your cat's diet by adding eggshell powder, bone meal, or calcium carbonate. Some raw foods activist owners prefer bone meal because it also includes an appropriate level of phosphorous. However, bone meal may not be good for cats with urinary problems, because it may contribute to crystals and other urinary tract health concerns, and because it does have a greater potential to be contaminated with toxins and bacteria. As far as calcium carbonate goes, the amount of usable calcium in calcium carbonate is much lower than that of either eggshells or bone meal, so you will need to use a larger amount of it.

Preparing cooked meals

Cooking for your cat is not unlike cooking for humans; only there will be no options to have steak cooked rare, medium, or well. Beef that is not thoroughly cooked always has a risk of becoming contaminated with bacteria. You will not need to burn your food, though. In fact, charred food actually contains carcinogens that you do not want to feed your cat (or yourself for that matter).

Meats that are sautéed can be done in a pan sprayed with a little non-stick spray. Although, most of those sprays are made from vegetable grains, the amount that adheres to the food is negligible enough not to be an area of concern. You can also bake, broil, steam, poach, and boil the meat. Steaming, poaching and boiling allow for a moister end product than either baking or broiling, which may be more preferable to your cat. The other methods produce a dryer food and may need to have broth or water added to it before feeding to your cat. A side benefit of boiling is that the water used to cook the foods will retain many of the vitamins that were cooked out of them. You can then use that water as a nutritious means of moistening meats that were possibly cooked in a dryer way.

Regardless of how the meat is cooked, unless your tom is semi-feral and spends quite a bit of time outdoors hunting and eating prey, he or she may not be used to the concept of eating chunks of meat. If your cat is used to roaming the neighborhood for tasty mice, he or she will know just how to handle a large piece of meat. However, if he is a housebound cat, he or she may not even realize it is food. Therefore, you will need to finely chop the food up or mince it to make it more familiar and encourage your cat to eat it. You may even want to grind the cooked meat or pulverize it in a food processor. Should you decide you want to offer small chunks, you will need to cut them into bite-sized pieces that will easily fit into your cat's mouth — think of it as kitty-bite size. To make cutting raw meat into tiny pieces easier, freeze it, and then let it thaw just enough to get a sharp knife through it. You will find semi-frozen meat is easier to handle than completely thawed.

As far as vegetables and the other carbohydrates go, those, too, will need to be in small pieces. You will also need to be aware of how long you are cooking the vegetables. The longer they cook, the more nutrients are lost. If you are cooking them in water to make a broth, then you do not have to worry about any vitamins or minerals escaping, as they will end up in the broth. But if you are baking the vegetables into a casserole or a loaf, you may want to be sure you give your tom a good multivitamin that day to make up for any missed nutrition.

Once the food is cooked and cooled enough to be stored, you can freeze it in individual servings as just described. Be sure you date the bags, and that you remember what day you put them in the refrigerator to thaw. Cats can suffer from food poisoning just as easily as humans can. Keep the cooked foods in their sealed containers, and use them quickly. Cooked foods left in the refrigerator for longer than four days, or that have an odd odor, should not be fed to your cat.

Time to Cook

· ·

Before you get started on any of the recipes, it might be a good idea to take stock of what you have on hand in your kitchen. Cooking for your cat is a simple process compared to cooking for your family. Because most of the food you will prepare will be fresh meats and produce, you will have very little need for spices and other food staples to be stored in your pantry. Aside from a meat grinder, you will only need basic kitchen gadgets and tools. There will be a minimum of skills to acquire or use in the preparation process. However, in case you are new to the kitchen, or are feeling a little insecure about preparing foods for your kitty, take a few minutes to go over what might be good to have available or know how to use before you start to tackle the recipes.

Staple Food Ingredients

You will find a few items are indispensable to have on hand at all times when preparing food for your cat (as well as for the human members of the pride). These are all easily found in most supermarket grocery stores, and even in the larger discount department stores. And for the most part, they do not need to be stored in the refrigerator. Although many will be in cans or otherwise sealed containers, do be sure to check for expiration dates, particularly if you purchase organic products or products labeled "no preservatives."

- **Broth:** You can make your own broth, of course, by cooking cat-safe vegetables or meats in water. If you make your own, you will need to store it in the freezer or refrigerator. Otherwise, prepared broths are available in the soup aisles of your supermarket. The only word of caution is to be sure to check the ingredients thoroughly. You will not want to give your cat broth that contains salt, artificial colors or flavors, onions, or garlic.

- **Eggs:** The best eggs will be from chickens raised humanely. Their cartons will be marked "cage free." Those eggs will be slightly more expensive than regular, but if you really care about animals, you must be aware of the horrible living conditions poultry is forced to suffer for their short lives just to produce eggs. Eggs can also be a good source of omega-3 fatty acids, too, as you can easily find cage-free eggs from chickens fed a diet supplemented with healthy fats in your supermarket.

- **Fats:** Again, you will not want to use margarine, solid or liquid vegetable oils, or lard for your cat. Margarine and the vegetable oils often contain grains your cat should not eat, and lard is usually preserved with potentially dangerous chemicals. The best fats to keep available are fish oils (including fish liver oils), which can be found in the supplement section of the market, and rendered chicken or goose fat, which you can make yourself *(see Supplement and Accompaniments Section of Recipes for instructions)*. Of course, the fat that is inherent in the bear, rabbit, or other meats you feed your kitty are just fine, too, but they are not as easily storable.

- **Rice:** Rice is a great, nourishing, and easily digestible grain for your cat. You can use it in many of the recipes in this book, but you should also keep it on hand if your kitty has an upset stomach or is recovering from a medical condition. Rice easily takes on the flavor of broths, so it will be palatable for even the pickiest palate and is one of the least allergenic foods in the world.

A Few Notes on Meats

Chicken is chicken is chicken, right? And the same goes for beef, correct? Well, not exactly. When it comes to purchasing poultry and meats, things are not always what they seem. Simply cooking them in ways to bring out their better quality can enhance different cuts of meat or types of poultry. These same ideas can be applied to cooking for the humans at the dinner table as well as for the kitty at your feet.

- **Chicken:** Did you realize that when you buy chicken at the market it is classified by its age and weight? Cornish hens are not necessarily a different chicken species, but one that has at least a little bit of Cornish DNA in it. Mostly it just lets you know it is a very young hen, hence its smaller size, weighing between one and 1 ½ pounds. A fryer is the same thing as a broiler; those names both refer to a youngish bird anywhere between 49 to 56 days old, weighing between 2 ½ to 4 ½ pounds. Roasters are a couple of weeks older than fryers and broilers, which explains why they are larger, and usually are between five and six pounds.

  When cooking chicken, the younger the bird, the tenderer the meat. Likewise, the older the bird, the tougher it is. What that means is, when you are cooking, you cannot chop up a roaster and plan to cook it lightly and quickly, as in sautéing. It will not be as tender as it would be if you cooked it slowly in the oven.

- **Turkey:** Fryer and roaster turkeys are between four and eight pounds. Fully mature turkeys can weigh up to 30 pounds. The same cooking advice applies to them as it does to chickens — the younger the bird, the tenderer it will be, and the less cooking time will be required for it. A bonus of using turkey is that, because it has a higher ratio of meat to bone than chickens do, it is generally more economical to purchase.

- **Duck and goose:** If something is labeled "duckling" it should only be three to four pounds. It will be very tender, even delicate, when you cook it, so frying or broiling will be fine. Older ducks usually weigh between five and six pounds, and geese are between eight and 16 pounds. Both require longer and gentler cooking, such as roasting or braising.

- **Beef:** Whether cut of beef is tender depends more on how the animal was raised than it does on the age at which it was slaughtered. Although, it does stand to reason, an older animal does produce a tougher cut of meat. You can tell the quality of meat by the look of it. Look for a bright, pink-red color. If bones are present in the cut, they should be light-colored and the fat should be white. The more "marbling" the appearance, that is, the more fat that can be seen in crooked lines or something akin to the veins in marble stone, the better the flavor and tenderer the meat. Cuts with more marbling are somewhat self-basting, as the fat melts during the cooking process and goes into the meat. The tenderer the cut of beef, the less time it needs to cook. The tougher cuts will need to cook longer to make them tender.

The vast majority of cattle on the market are fed grains to get fatter more quickly before they are slaughtered. The meats they produce are of inferior quality to those that are labeled "grass-fed." Though grass-fed beef may be slightly gamier in taste, it does provide some omega-3 fatty acids grain-fed cows do not; so, in that sense, the nutritional quality is better. Because grass-fed cows eat foods that are more natural for them

— cows are like cats and do not tolerate grains — eating grass-fed beef, and serving it to your cat is more environmentally friendly because to provide grain for cattle, crops must be harvested and processed — two industrialized methods that require energy resources of oil and gas to power the machines and factories. Grass grows with the energy from the sun and rain in a meadow.

Veal is beef that comes from the calves, or babies, of cows. It is more expensive than regular beef. There is great controversy around the use of veal in that the animals are often housed in poor living quarters, and their lives are cut down to a very short existence. Veal comes from animals that are not even weaned from their mother's milk yet. There is no nutrition in veal that your cat cannot get from regular beef. You can comfortably forgo feeding veal to your cat for more humanely treated animals, knowing he or she will not be missing out on any vital nutrition.

- **Lamb:** Lamb comes from the meat of sheep that are younger than one year. In Europe, mutton, which is an older sheep, is eaten, but it is not widely found in the United States. The tenderist kind of lamb is called "spring lamb" because it was once only available from March through September. But because it is now relatively easy to transport meats around the world, sheep grown in Australia and New Zealand are available during the spring months for those countries, which happens to be during the fall and winter in the northern hemisphere. There are winter lambs (from both hemispheres), and their meat is generally tougher. A leg from a spring lamb weighs between four and seven pounds; a winter lamb leg can get as large as nine pounds. Similar to beef, when purchasing lamb meat, look for bright pinkish-red meat, pink bones, and white fat. And remember, the younger the lamb (the spring lambs), the tenderer the meat.

As far as other meats go, their tenderness will be determined by whether or not they are game meat, that is, meat that can only be obtained from hunting. Rabbit was once considered game meat, but now it is often sold in supermarkets. Rabbit meat tastes similar to chicken, though it is dryer. You can substitute rabbit for chicken in many recipes, but be sure to increase the moisture content for your cat. Venison, bison, and buffalo are all game types of meat, which some cats prefer to the more domestic animals. You can only get venison if you know a hunter or are a hunter. It is very tough in texture and will need to be cooked a long while for your cat to be able to comfortably chew it. Bison and buffalo are sometimes sold in specialty meat stores and natural food markets.

You will notice that recipes calling for mice, rats, and other rodents are missing from this book. If you wish to use those to feed your cat, you will need to find a supplier either online or via a pet store. Many pet stores keep them in freezers to give to the owners of snakes, since snakes need to eat them. Cooking them is not suggested; their bodies are so small, it depletes the nutrients almost completely. So, unless you are going to provide your cat with frozen mouse and rat bodies, you may just want to stick to the more readily available foods.

In the Resources Section of this book, you will find a brief list of online companies that can and will provide raw meats to feed your cat. Those meats run the gamut from whole fowl and beef to fish and other sea creatures. They will come with instructions on the thawing, handling, and preparations needed to feed them to your cat.

Handy Kitchen Tools and Utensils

You probably already have most of the following items on hand in your kitchen. Because the food ingredients are the same sources you use for the rest of the family, you will not need to buy separate ones for your kitty, nor store them in separate areas of the house out of fear that they may somehow contaminate the human supplies. The following list is not exhaustive, but should cover the needs of preparing the foods in the Recipe Section of this book.

- **Measuring cups:** It is important that you have two sets of measuring cups: one for dry ingredients and one for wet ones. For dry ingredients, you will usually need to have a set of different cups in graduated sizes: ⅛ cup, ¼ cup, ⅓ cup, ½ cup, and 1 cup will cover most needs. Each can be filled to heaping and then leveled off with the backside of a knife or other flat item to create a perfectly measured amount. For liquids, find a measuring cup with a spout to make the liquid easier to pour. Usually a liquid measuring cup is only one item with hash marks indicating how much of the ingredient is in the cup.

- **Measuring spoons:** A good measuring spoon set has a graduated series of spoons measuring out ⅛ teaspoon, ¼ teaspoon, ½ teaspoon, 1 teaspoon, and 1 tablespoon. You will find the 1- tablespoon size to be indispensable when measuring out serving sizes for your kitty, so you may wish to invest in a heavy-duty metal set that will last for years of repeated use.

- **Meat thermometer:** If you are not making raw meals for your cat, you will need to be sure the meat you use is cooked thoroughly. It is imperative that you cook meats to a temperature that will kill off any potential bacteria and make your foods safe to eat. The following chart depicts the minimum internal cooking temperatures as recommended by the United States Department of Agriculture:

Food Item	Cooking Temperature
Beef, veal, lamb	160° F – 165° F
Chicken, turkey and other fowl	165° F
Fish	145° F
Eggs	160° F
Reheated leftover foods	165° F

- **Timer:** For most of the recipes, the timer on your stove or oven will probably be sufficient. However, if decide to take on cooking jerky for your cat, your timer may not go up to the three- to six-hour mark, and you will need to rely on another one.

- **Bowls:** A good set of mixing bowls or at least three different sizes will be indispensable. Stainless steel, glass, and glazed earthenware are best as plastic can become scored and scratched by sharp utensils. Those bits of damage can become hiding places and breeding grounds for bacteria that can later cause food poisoning.

- **Chopping board:** The debate about which is safer — wooden or acrylic chopping boards — is ongoing. Some believe that the wood will absorb and store germs, and others say that the acrylic, once scratched, will do the same. Regardless of which style you use, to be safe, always remember to clean the chopping board with a disinfecting soap to prevent food poisoning.

- **Knives:** A good set of sharp, stainless steel, or carbon steel knives are a must. Stainless steel will not rust, but the carbon steel will stay sharper longer. You must have heavy-duty knives that can cut through bone. You will also need to have a knife sharpener or whetting stone and use it frequently. Bones can be very dulling to a knife blade.

- **Grater:** Graters are perfect for making vegetables easier for your cat to digest because they break down the more fibrous parts of the vegetable.

- **Poultry shears:** If your kitty has a special liking for chicken, you may want to invest in a good set of poultry shears. They are made specifically for cutting through chicken bones.

- **Meat grinder:** If you intend to feed your cat raw foods on a regular basis, a meat grinder is a must.

- **Meat pounder:** This item may not be necessary most of the time, but if your cat ever is having any kind of tooth problem, pounding the meats before you feed them to her will make them tenderer and easier to chew.

- **Pots, pans, and skillets:** You will need these items to cook. At the minimum you should have on hand: a good 10-inch skillet or frying pan with a cover, a tall stockpot large enough to hold an entire chicken or couple of pounds of meat with liquid, and a four- to six-quart pot with a lid.

- **Wooden spoons/mixing spoons:** Wooden spoons share the same bad reputation as wooden chopping boards — there is a fear that they can house dangerous food toxins. However, they do not melt, they do not damage non-stick cookware, and they do not conduct heat; so, you never risk burning your hand. If you use wooden spoons, just be sure to properly disinfect them with a disinfecting soap or spray after each use.

- **Rubber spatula:** Nothing works as well as a rubber spatula to scrape a bowl clean, but you cannot use it on hot skillets, because it will melt.

- **Bulb baster:** Your cat's food needs to be moist and nothing helps meat stay moist better than basting it frequently when you are cooking it in an oven.

- **Fish poacher:** Fish poachers can be used for other meats besides fish. It is a great method for keeping meats moist when cooking on the stove.

- **Electric Crock-pot®:** Another method of cooking moist meats is to use a slow cooker or Crock-pot. It will also help ensure the meat is tender, hence, easier to chew for older cats or cats with teeth and gum issues.

- **Rolling pin:** A large, heavy pin is best for rolling out the dough to make cat treats. Most of the dough contains meats and denser items than human pie or cookie dough, so you will need a heftier pin unless you have very strong biceps.

- **Loaf pans:** A few of the recipes here call for using a loaf pan. They come in two standard sizes: 9 x 5 x 3 inches and 8 ½ x 4 ½ x 2 ½ inches. If your cat likes crunchier foods, use the larger size as the foods will be thinner when they cook. If your cat prefers moister foods, the smaller size will make them thicker.

- **Cake pans and roasting pan:** A cake pan and large roasting pans will be handy for cooking large fowl, rabbits, and other larger pieces of meat. You can also use it as a poacher of sorts, putting water in it and then setting a loaf pan filled with food in the water. The steam that is released from the water will help the food keep moist.

- **Dutch oven:** A Dutch oven is a heavy cooking pot with a tight-fitting lid that you can place in the oven and bake at high temperatures. It is yet another method of cooking moist meats.

- **Cookie sheets:** Will be useful for baking treats.

- **Ramekins:** These small bowls are often sold with lids. They are perfect for recipes that require small amounts of food, in the case of cat food that would be the vegetables and cat-friendly grains. You can premeasure the ingredients into the ramekins so that when it is time to add to the dish you are preparing, you do not have to stop and measure, but just pour.

- **Food processor:** Many of the recipes will call for you to process or pulverize ingredients, and for that, a food processors is the best tool to use. It is also particularly good for finely chopping, grating, grinding, and pureeing. Not all food processors are created equal when it comes to evenly processing the ingredients. You risk having some of the finished product more processed than other parts of it if you do not cater to the way your machine works. With some processors, you will need to slowly feed the food into the unit as it runs, rather than just filling the bowl and hitting the "on" button. For other processors, you will need to continually hit the "on" and "off" button to make the machine pulse.

- **Storage containers:** Because you will be making several meals at one time for your cat, you really need to figure out ahead of time how you will store them. Resealable bags may seem ideal in that they come in a variety of sizes and are relatively inexpensive, but please remember the impact they have on the environment. Unless you plan on cleaning them and reusing them, they will be going directly into a landfill. Consider purchasing containers you can keep in the freezer.

You may already have many of the above referenced items in your kitchen cupboards (where some cats are probably hiding now), particularly if you are already comfortable cooking and experimenting in the kitchen. If not, nearly everything can be conveniently purchased at kitchen supply stores like Williams-Sonoma or Bed Bath and Beyond. You can even find them at the larger discount department stores, such as Target or Walmart.

Kitchen Skills and Terms

If you are comfortable in the kitchen, you may want to just skip this section. However, if you are still finding your way around the room to prepare human foods, you might pick up a handy tip or two here, or at least learn the meaning of an unfamiliar term used in a recipe in this book.

- **Baste:** To baste something is to add moisture to it while it cooks. When basting meats, you can use a bulb baster, a large spoon, or a pastry brush to periodically apply broth, fat, or cooking juices to the top of the meat.

- **Beat:** To beat ingredients, you need to mix them together rapidly, incorporating air into them, until they form a smooth mixture. Beating by hand is best done with a whisk or fork.

- **Blanch:** Blanching means you cook something in rapidly boiling water for a brief period, sometimes for less than minute. You do not blanch an item to cook it thoroughly; rather you do it to jump-start the cooking process for something you will bake or to just soften the food enough to eat with ease without stripping it of its nutrients, color, or flavor.

- **Blend:** Blending differs from beating in that it is more of a gentle mixing of ingredients. Also, you usually only blend two items together at one time, whereas you can beat several together at once.

- **Braise:** To braise a food, you cook it covered in liquid for a long period.

- **Broil:** Cooking on a grill or in an oven with very hot heat source set above the food.

- **Brown:** To brown something is to cook it under a broiler or sear it in a frying pan just enough to change the color of the meat to brown. In essence, it seals in the moisture of the meat, and it is often the first step in making a stew. When you brown something, it is best to make sure the outside of the meat is dry (use a paper towel to absorb excess water if necessary) and turn the item while it is on the heat source so each side is equally brown.

- **Chop versus dice:** When you cut up a solid item by taking a knife using a rocking motion until the item is in small pieces, you are chopping. If you take the time to make several slices in one direction and then turn the item to make several slices in a different direction so that you end up with little cubes of food, you are dicing.

- **Drippings:** The fat, juices, and browned bits that collect in the pot or roasting pan when cooking meat are the drippings. If not used in the dish you are preparing at that instant, you may collect and freeze the drippings for use in other dishes later.

- **Fillet:** As a verb, when you fillet, you cut fish or meat so you remove the bones from the meat. The noun meaning refers to the meat that has had the bones removed from it.

- **Fry versus sauté:** Frying is a cooking method done with fat in a skillet or shallow pan. When you are using just a small amount of fat, and you stir your foods, you are sautéing. However, if you leave the food undisturbed — unless turning it over in the pan — you are frying, or deep-frying, depending on the amount of fat.

- **Knead:** To knead is to use your hands to push down, and then fold over, dough in a repeating fashion.

- **Mince:** Mincing creates the smallest pieces of cut up food you can make without using a food processor or grater.

- **Parboil:** Similar to blanching, only you leave the food in the boiling water for a little while longer. You cook it until it is almost, but not quite, done.

- **Poach:** Poaching is a very gentle simmering.

- **Roast:** To cook something with a dry heat, as in an oven, is to roast it.

- **Simmer:** To cook just under the point of boiling is to simmer.

- **Steep:** You steep something by pouring boiling liquid over it and letting it sit in the liquid.

Now that you are armed with a well-stocked pantry, a fully equipped kitchen, and a familiarity with the terms and techniques for cooking, you are ready to dig in and start preparing recipes for your cat. Start wherever you want, either by making a few side dishes to go with his or her current food or by making a complete meal as a special celebratory feast. If you know your cat has a particular like for a flavor of commercial cat food, it may be your guide as to where to start — if your cat loves a canned chicken product, chances are he or she will love a homemade chicken dish from you.

Recipes

It is finally time to get to the recipes! The following recipes are compiled with ingredients generally considered safe for cats to consume. However, common sense rules apply here — if your cat has an allergy or intolerance to a particular ingredient, substitute it with one he or she can handle. Make substitutions to accommodate particular health issues, such as using chicken to replace the beef in recipes for cats with chronic renal failure. You can also substitute ingredients your cat likes for ones he or she does not like. Just remember, you must always substitute like for like — if your cat does not like chicken, substitute another meat for it, and do not use a carbohydrate or fat source. Also, be sure to keep the ratios of total calories consumed at the 60 percent protein, 30 percent fat, and 10 percent carbohydrate ratio.

As far as serving the food itself goes, kittens seem to prefer their food on the warm side, perhaps because the food is more like their mother's milk, which is on the warm side. The cardinal rule for human baby milk out of a bottle holds true for kittens — if you heat their food, test it on the inside of your wrist to be sure it is not too hot. If it feels uncomfortable or burns the thin skin on your wrist, it can burn the inside of a kitten's mouth. However, most adult cats do not have a preference for one food temperature over another. Some will refuse to eat extremely cold food. Perhaps that is because they have never had it, or maybe it is an atavistic repulsion, as your cat's wild ancestors never ate anything that came out of a refrigerator. Or maybe she just knows that humans occasionally eat frozen TV dinners, and she thinks you are trying to make her stoop to that level; you may probably never know the real reason.

Each of these recipes will make several serving sizes of food for your cat. You will need to store them as you do human food. Even if the food is cooked, it must be refrigerated, or you risk bacterial contamination and spoilage. It is probably a good idea to label and date the containers of food so you know exactly what is in them and how long they have been in the refrigerator. Refrigerated food can usually be kept safe for three to four days. If you do not think you can use all the food within that time frame, you should freeze it immediately upon making it. *Refer back to Chapter 8 for tips and ideas regarding freezing your homemade cat food and treats.*

Creating Supplements & Accompaniments

This section provides recipes on creating supplements or accompaniments you can use to increase a particular vitamin or mineral content in your cat's meals, to address a temporary health condition, or to feed alongside a meat-only meal. Some supplements, such as the ground eggshells, you may find yourself using every day, as it is a convenient source of calcium. Other supplements, you may want to serve on an occasional basis. For example, rice can be used as a side dish to a meat meal, or used by itself as a small, easily digestible meal for a kitty that has been under the weather and does not feel up to eating a full, heavy meal.

Recipe 1: Ground eggshells

If you are feeding your cat raw meats and grinding the bones, remember you may not need to add calcium to the diet, because it will come from the bones. However, if you are feeding your cat cooked foods, you cannot give him or her bones because they will become too brittle in the cooking process, so you will need to add calcium to meals. One jumbo egg makes about one teaspoon of ground eggshells, which will provide about 1,800 mg of usable calcium. An adult cat should get around 1,000 mg calcium every day for strong bones.

Ingredients:
- Eggshells

You will also need:
- Baking sheets
- Sifter

Directions:
1. There are two methods of obtaining eggshells that are free of bacteria.

   a. The first is to save the shells removed from hard-boiled eggs. Rinse the shells very well, and allow them to air dry.

   b. The second is, after cracking an uncooked egg, rinse the shell pieces thoroughly and arrange in a single layer on a baking sheet. It is important that they are not piled on top of each other, because you risk the center of the piles not baking long enough to kill off bacteria. Bake the shells in a 300° F oven for 10 minutes.

2. With either the boiled or baked method, when shells are clean and dry, place in blender or food processor, and grind until there are no sharp pieces. The end product should look like a powder.

3. Sift the powder to remove large, sharp pieces.

Note: Ground eggshells last indefinitely as long as they stay dry in a sealed container.

Recipe 2: Liver, as you want it

Liver has necessary trace minerals and vitamins and the ever-needed taurine, but too much of it is not a good thing, as feeding large amounts to your cat on a daily basis can lead to a toxicity of other minerals. The recipe below is for cooked liver. If you are serving raw-only foods, you simply grind the raw liver before freezing it. Because cooking depletes nutrients, raw liver will have more nutrition than cooked, so you may want to feed it even more sparingly. After you prepare the liver by grinding — or as the directions instruct — you can freeze it in 1-tablespoon serving sizes in small, sealable plastic bags. Pull a bag out, and thaw whenever you want to add the liver to another recipe or give it to your kitty for a special treat.

Ingredients:

- Liver (chicken, beef, veal, turkey, or any other feline-stomach friendly source)

Directions:

1. Bring enough water in a pan to completely cover the liver to a boil over high heat.

2. Chop the liver into tiny (i.e., bite-sized for a kitty's mouth) pieces.

3. Boil liver for 15 minutes.

4. Drain, measure out into individual serving sizes, and store.

Recipe 3: Rendered chicken or duck fat

Chicken or duck fat will come in handy when you need to cook meat that is leaner or tougher than you really want to feed your cat. You can add it in when cooking, or heat it up alone and drizzle over the top. It might also be a good idea to try to use it when encouraging kitty to try a vegetable or grain, as it will give the food more of a meat taste.

Ingredients:

- Chicken or duck, both entire birds, or just bird parts will do. You do not need to buy a separate bird for this. You can remove the fat from the various birds you use in other recipes and store it in the freezer until you have a large amount to render, which will be about one cup.

Directions:

1. Remove the fat off the birds. You will want to use the obvious, yellow fat. On whole birds, you will find the area around the tail to be the most plentiful.

2. Cut the fat into small pieces, less than 1-inch square. Cutting it when still frozen will be easiest, as it will handle better and be more stable under your knife.

3. Set the fat into a large skillet, and cook over low heat until it melts, and the pieces remaining are crispy and brown.

4. Remove the pieces, and allow them to drain on a paper towel (these will be special treats for your cat, or you can add them in with other foods as extra bits of flavor).

5. The remaining fat in the skillet will be the rendered fat.

Note: You can store the rendered fat in an airtight jar in your refrigerator indefinitely.

Recipe 4: Vegetables on the ready

Precooked, stewed vegetables can be measured and stored just as easily as liver. Keep them separated by type or mix together into a goulash to have anything you might want handy. Variations are endless with this recipe, as you can mix the vegetables and the broths you decide to cook them in. If you are serving only raw foods to your kitty, the vegetables will need to be ground as finely as possible before freezing. The ice-cube tray method of freezing works well here, as the serving sizes are so small.

Ingredients:

- 1 cup of chopped and diced vegetables per cup of broth
- Safe vegetables, such as peeled white potatoes, peas, pumpkin, zucchini, squashes, broccoli, Brussels sprouts, or green beans *(see Chapter 1 for more suggestions)*
- Meat-based broths, such as beef, chicken, turkey, fish (If using packaged, store-bought broths, be sure there are no unsafe additives for flavoring, such as onion or garlic.)

Directions:

1. Cook the vegetables in simmering broth until tender.
2. Drain the vegetables, but not completely; remember your cat's food needs to remain moist.
3. Divide into 1-tablespoon serving sizes and freeze.

Recipe 5: Any-flavor rice

Because rice is so easily digestible, it makes a great source of carbohydrates for 5 to 10 percent of your cat's diet. If your cat will not turn his or her nose up at it, brown rice will provide needed fiber, too.

Ingredients:

- 1 cup rice
- 2 cups broth, any flavor

Directions:

1. Bring the broth to a boil.

2. Pour in the rice, and return to a boil.

3. Cover pot with tight lid, reduce heat, and simmer 20 minutes.

4. If cooking with brown rice, your simmer time may need to be doubled.

5. A special note regarding cooking rice: It will become sticky if you lift the lid to peek and see if it is done prior to it actually being done. Try to refrain from checking on it until the allotted time is over.

Recipe 6: Herbal Teas

Sometimes, with your veterinarian's approval, you may want to give a kitty that is feeling a little under the weather a special herb to make him or her feel better. You can make a tea out of it and pour it over her kibble or other meals for him or her to lap it up along with the regular food. The tea can also be used to add parsley, basil, oregano, and other herbs for additional green nutrition.

Other herbs and their uses include:

- **Bugleweed:** Helps control an overactive thyroid
- **Quackgrass** (also called Couch grass): Serves as a good remedy for urinary tract inflammation
- **Hawthorn** (Crataegus species): Used with cats suffering from heart conditions
- **Nettle** (Urtica species): Serves as a supplement providing protein and trace minerals
- **Milk Thistle:** Helps the liver stay healthy
- **Peppermint:** Helps relieve an indigestion and upset stomachs

Ingredients:

- 1 to 2 teaspoons dried herbs or 2 to 4 tablespoons chopped fresh
- 1 cup boiling water

Directions:

1. Steep the herbs for 5 to 6 minutes, then drain.
2. Allow tea to cool to room temperature before pouring over your cat's food.

Treats

The recipes in this section are not to be used as an everyday meal. They are for the special occasion, maybe to reward kitty when finally managing to stay away from the potted fern for the entire day. Some of these treats will be heavy on meat ingredients, providing more protein calories for the day, and others will be heavier on the vegetable and grains, which will provide more carbohydrate calories. Be sure to consider the treat calories, as you may need to feed your cat a little less at dinner if he or she had a large treat in the middle of the afternoon.

Recipe 7: Dried jerky treats

This recipe might seem like a long process, but there is little labor involved and because it stores for so long, you can make a large amount of it and always have some readily on hand. If you have a food dehydrator at home or a newer digital oven with a "dehydrator" setting, you may already be familiar with making homemade beef or venison jerky. Alternatively, some microwave ovens are fitted for dehydrating meat and vegetables and may be used instead of a conventional oven. If using either, please refer to your product's instructions for timetable adjustments.

Ingredients:

- Choice of meats — chicken (breast, thighs, liver, heart), beef (brisket, flank, sandwich, skirt or round steak, liver), venison (front shoulders or cuts similar to beef cuts)

Directions:

1. Preheat oven on lowest setting (150° F is ideal).

2. Slice the meat against the grain into strips no wider than ⅛ inch. It is easier to cut uniform, thin strips if you freeze the meat first, but freeze it just enough to make it firm. Do not leave it in the freezer so long that it becomes a solid chunk too hard to cut.

3. Remove oven racks and line the bottom of the oven with foil to catch

drippings. Spray racks with non-stick spray and return to the oven.

4. Arrange meat strips horizontally across the racks. Leave approximately ½-inch space between meat pieces to allow air to circulate between them.

5. Bake with the oven door just slightly ajar for about 3 hours. You are not "cooking" the meat, but drying it out, the door will need to remain open to allow the moisture in the meat to escape the oven. Otherwise, it builds up as steam and will make the meat stay too moist.

6. The jerky is done when the meat is shriveled, dry, and — when you bend it — gives way without breaking. Depending on the type of meat and the amount of moisture in the ambient air, it could take as long as 6 hours.

7. Completely dehydrated jerky can last for up to two years if stored in a cool, dark place. Though you can keep it frozen, taking out a few pieces at a time to thaw for your cat.

8. If your cat has trouble chewing on the jerky and is not interested in the exercise it gives her teeth, you may want to cut it up into kitty-bite-sized pieces to serve.

Recipe 8: Holy mackerel bites

Ingredients:

- 1 8-ounce can of mackerel fish (found alongside tuna at your market)
- 4 tablespoons finely chopped fresh catnip
- 1 teaspoon ground eggshells
- 2 ½ cups oat flour
- 3 eggs, beaten

Directions:

1. Preheat oven to 375° F
2. With a fork, mash the mackerel until fine.
3. Mix all other ingredients in with the mackerel until dough forms.
4. Create a ball out of the dough and remove to a flat surface.
5. Roll out the dough to ¼-inch thick.
6. Cut into ½-inch squares, or use small cookie cutters to cut fun shapes.
7. Bake the bites at 375° F for 20 to 25 minutes. The longer the baking time, the crunchier the bites. So, bake to your kitty's preference.

Recipe 9: Better-than-ever mackerel treats

Ingredients:

- 1 tablespoon fish liver oil
- 1 egg
- 1 cup whole oats
- 1 8-ounce can of mackerel, drained

Directions:

1. Preheat oven to 350° F.
2. Using a fork, break up the mackerel in a mixing bowl.
3. Add in whole oats, fish liver oil, and egg.
4. Drop by ½ teaspoonful onto a cookie sheet covered with non-stick spray.
5. Bake for 8 to 10 minutes.

Recipe 10: Salmon balls

Ingredients:

- 12 ounce can salmon
- 1 egg
- 1 cup whole oats

Directions:

1. Preheat oven to 350° F.

2. In a food processor or blender, pulverize the whole oats until mealy and crumbly, then set aside.

3. Next in the food processor, combine salmon and egg, and process until creamy.

4. Pour mixture into a mixing bowl.

5. Stir in pulverized oats until well combined and mixture is staying together.

6. Form small balls.

7. Drop onto cookie sheet covered with non-stick spray.

8. Bake for 15 minutes.

Recipe 11: Savory sardines

Ingredients:

- 2 cans flat sardines in oil
- 1 chicken liver, pureed
- ½ to 1 cup cooked rolled oats

Directions:

1. Smash sardines with a fork.

2. Mix sardines and chicken liver until well blended.

3. Stir in the rolled oats until you have a consistency that will allow you to roll the mixture into small balls.

Recipe 12: Savory sardines II

Ingredients:

- 1 can sardines in oil
- ⅓ cup carrots, cooked and chopped
- ¼ cup rye grass, finely chopped
- ⅓ cup cooked rice

Directions:

1. Empty sardine tin into food processor.
2. Pulse and blend until smooth.
3. Combine rice, carrots, and catnip in a mixing bowl.
4. Pour in sardine mixture, blending together.
5. Keep refrigerated and spoon out whenever kitty would like a special treat.

Recipe 13: The best chicken liver balls

Ingredients:

- 1 ½ pound chicken livers
- 1 cup whole oats
- ¾ cup rice flour
- ¼ cup chicken broth, more if needed
- 2 large eggs, beaten

Directions:

1. Preheat oven to 350° F.
2. In a blender or food processor, pulverize whole oats until mealy and crumbly.
3. Brown the chicken livers in frying pan. Remove, and allow them to cool to the touch.
4. Finely chop the chicken livers.
5. Mix chicken livers with remaining ingredients to create dough.
6. Aim for a stiff dough, but not too dry. If mixture will not hold together, add more broth.

7. Form dough into marble-sized balls, and place on cookie sheet covered with non-stick spray.

8. With basting brush, brush more broth onto dough balls.

9. Bake for 8 to 10 minutes.

Recipe 14: Tasty chicken liver and veggie bites

Ingredients:

- 2 cups rice flour
- 1 cup whole oats
- 1 egg
- 3 tablespoons chicken fat or fish liver oil
- ½ cup chicken broth
- 1 tablespoon chopped, fresh parsley
- 1 cup diced, cooked chicken livers
- 1 cup cooked mixed vegetables

Directions

1. Preheat oven to 400° F.

2. Pulverize oats in a food processor or blender

3. Combine rice flour and pulverized whole oats in a mixing bowl.

4. In another bowl, blend the egg with the oil.

5. Slowly add the broth and parsley to egg and oil mixture.

6. Add the dry mix to the wet ingredients, stirring while adding.

7. Stir in chicken livers, making sure to evenly distribute.

8. Combine well to form dough

9. On a board covered with rice flour, knead the dough until it forms a ball.

10. Roll out to ½-inch thick.

11. Cut into ¼-inch squares, or use small cookie cutters to cut shapes.

12. Bake for 10 to 12 minutes.

Recipe 15: Chicken liver surprises

Ingredients:

- 1 pound chicken livers
- ⅓ cup water
- ¼ cup carrots, grated
- 1 cup rice flour
- ¼ cup oat flour
- 1 tablespoon melted chicken fat or fish liver oil

Directions:

1. Preheat oven to 350° F.
2. Cook chicken livers in frying pan. Allow to cool before handling.
3. Pulverize chicken livers in food processor.
4. Add in water and carrots, and blend until smooth and somewhat pasty.
5. Move to mixing bowl, and add in the rice flour and oat flour, mixing well.
6. Add the melted fat as needed to keep dough together and so that it has a sticky feel to it.
7. Cover board with rice flour, and roll out the sticky dough onto it until ¼-inch thick.
8. Cut into 1-inch-sized pieces, or use a small cookie cutter.
9. Place on cookie sheet well covered with a non-stick spray.
10. Bake 7 minutes. Flip, and bake another 5 to 6 more minutes, until golden brown.

Recipe 16: Chicken pâté

Just like the delicacy humans enjoy, pâté can be served as a special treat to your cat.

Ingredients:

- 4 pieces of chicken innards (You can ask your butcher to set some aside for you, but often they are packaged inside whole roasters.)
- 6 ounce chicken livers
- 1 ounce chicken fat, melted
- 1 egg
- 1 tablespoon fresh parsley, finely chopped

Directions:

1. Preheat oven to 350° F.
2. Rinse hearts, gizzards, and livers, then pat dry.
3. Cook chicken parts in the chicken fat until brown, and allow cooling.
4. Process all chicken parts in a food processor, or blend in a blender.
5. Add the egg, and puree.
6. Cover loaf pan with non-stick cooking spray.
7. Fill loaf pan with pâté mixture.
8. Place loaf pan onto a large roasting pan.
9. Pour about 2 inches of boiling water into the roasting pan; be careful not to go over the sides of the loaf pan and enter the pâté.
10. Bake with the loaf pan in the water for 30 minutes.
11. Allow cooling prior to removing from loaf pan.
12. Pâté may be kept in the freezer for long storage, but you may want to keep some thawed in the refrigerator so that kitty always has a special treat available for her.

Recipe 17: Beef liver bites

Ingredients:

- 1 pound beef liver
- 1 cup whole oats
- 1 ½ cups rice flour
- 1 teaspoon water

Directions:

1. Preheat oven to 350° F.
2. In a blender or food processor, pulverize the whole oats until mealy and crumbly. Set aside.
3. Process the liver in the food processor until mushy.
4. Add the rice flour, pulverized whole oats, and water to the liver in the processor, and pulse the machine until all is mixed thoroughly.
5. Spray cookie sheet with non-stick spray.
6. Spread out liver mix onto the cookie sheet, pressing down to remove air pockets.
7. Bake for 20 minutes.
8. Let cool and cut into kitty-bite-sized pieces.

Recipe 18: Autumn harvest treats

Ingredients:

- ¾ cup canned pumpkin (not pie filling)
- 2 eggs
- 2 cups pulverized whole oats
- ⅓ cup crushed sunflower seeds

Directions:

1. Preheat oven to 350° F.
2. Mix together canned pumpkin and eggs with a hand mixer or fast whisking.
3. Add in the pulverized oats and seeds, stirring well.
4. Spray 15 ½-inch by 10 ½-inch baking pan with non-stick spread.
5. Spread mixture into baking pan and bake 40 minutes.
6. Let cool and then cut into kitty-bite-sized pieces.

Recipe 19: Carrot cake for cats

Ingredients:

- 2 eggs
- ½ cup plain goat's-milk yogurt
- 3 tablespoons fish liver oil or melted fat
- ½ cup chicken broth
- 1 ½ cup rice flour
- 1 cup oat flour
- 1 cup shredded carrots

Directions:

1. Preheat oven to 400° F.
2. In large bowl, mix together eggs, yogurt, and oil.
3. In a different mixing bowl, mix flours together.
4. Slowly stir the dry ingredients into the wet.
5. Stir in the shredded carrots.
6. Cover a 9-inch cake pan with non-stick spray, dust with rice flour.
7. Pour in cake mixture.
8. Bake 40 to 45 minutes, or until toothpick inserted into the middle of the cake comes out clean.

Two-Ingredient Meals (Plus Supplements)

The following recipes are easy to prepare — meat and a vegetable with a sprinkling of eggshells and taurine. Of course, there is no need to limit yourself to what you find here. Let them serve as inspiration to experiment and find your cat's favorite combinations. If you wish, you can add hearts, livers, and gizzards to the meats for an even better quality of protein.

The flexibility with these recipes is endless. If you are planning to give your cat a raw-foods diet, you can change the amounts to 1 pound of meat and 2 tablespoons of vegetables. If you go raw, you can eliminate the need for added taurine by always including the innards.

Recipe 20: Turkey and pumpkin

Ingredients:

- 1 ½ pounds turkey, both light and dark meat
- 1 cup canned pumpkin
- 1 teaspoon powdered eggshells
- 1,000 mg taurine

Directions:

1. Boil turkey for 20 minutes. Drain and cool.
2. Finely mince the turkey.
3. Stir in pumpkin, eggshells, and taurine.

Recipe 21: Beef and broccoli

Ingredients:

- 1 ½ pounds ground beef
- 2 cups finely chopped broccoli
- 1 teaspoon powdered eggshells
- 1,000 mg taurine

Directions:

1. Brown the beef in a frying pan, but do not drain.
2. Meanwhile, lightly boil the broccoli, or steam it, until tender.
3. Mix beef and broccoli together.
4. Stir in eggshells and taurine.

Recipe 22: Lamb and collard greens

Ingredients:

- 1 ½ pounds lamb meat
- 2 cups greens (collard, kale Swiss Chard or dandelion)
- 1 teaspoon powdered eggshells
- 1,000 mg taurine

Directions:

1. Bake the lamb in 350° F oven for 25 minutes or until done. Alternately, you can use leftover leg of lamb, mutton, or other lamb cuts.
2. Meanwhile, blanch the greens.
3. In a food processor, pulverize the cooked lamb together with the greens.
4. Stir in eggshells and taurine.

Recipe 23: Venison and peas

Ingredients:

- 1 ½ pounds venison steak
- 2 cups peas
- 1 teaspoon powdered eggshells
- 1,000 mg taurine

Directions:

1. Fry the venison steak in a skillet. Allow cooling when done.
2. Thaw peas if already cooked, or blanch if they are raw.
3. Mince venison to the point where it looks shredded.
4. Stir peas in with the venison, adding water, if necessary, to keep moist.
5. Stir in the eggshells and taurine.

Recipe 24: Chicken and carrots

Ingredients:

- 1 ½ pounds chicken (alternately, use a Cornish game hen)
- 2 cups chopped carrots
- 1 teaspoon powdered eggshells
- 1,000 mg taurine

Directions:

1. Boil the chicken or hen. Drain, and allow cooling.
2. If necessary remove all the meat from the carcass of the game hen.
3. Blanch the chopped carrots, cooking until they are tender.
4. Finely chop the chicken or hen meat.
5. Mix in the carrots, eggshells, and taurine.

In-the-Raw Meat Meals

Many of the above recipes can be tweaked if you decide to go the raw route. Again, you will not need to add as much taurine into the mixtures of food, as cooking depletes that nutrient. There is also moistness inherent in most raw foods because of the juices naturally present in the meats, so you will probably not need to add any other liquid. However, if you find the food, upon thawing, looks as if it dried out some in the freezer, feel free to moisten with a little water or broth.

Recipe 25: Raw turkey-veggie mix

Ingredients:
- 1 pound ground turkey
- 4 turkey or chicken livers (mix of white and dark meats)
- ⅓ cup shredded carrots
- ⅓ cup canned pumpkin
- 1 teaspoon eggshell powder

Directions:
1. Puree livers with blender or food processor.
2. Mix livers with ground meat.
3. Mix in shredded carrots and pumpkin.
4. Stir in eggshell powder

Recipe 26: Everyday raw chicken

Ingredients:

- 1 whole chicken fryer with skin, giblets and all internal organs. Discard the neck unless you know your grinder can handle grinding bones.
- ¼ pound mixed, fresh vegetables
- 1 cup chicken broth
- 1 tablespoon fish liver oil
- 1,000 mg taurine
- 2 teaspoons eggshell powder

Directions:

1. Cut up the chicken at the joints, down the middle and across the back. Feed all into meat grinder.

2. Feed the gizzards and organs through the grinder; follow with the neck if you can and the vegetables.

3. Mix all ground meat and vegetables thoroughly. Add in chicken broth for moisture and the supplements. Again, mix thoroughly.

Recipe 27: The whole turkey

Save the innards from Thanksgiving or other family meals to use with this recipe.

Ingredients:

- 1 pound dark meat turkey
- Turkey innards (liver, heart, gizzards)
- ¼ cup shredded carrots or canned pumpkin
- 1 cup cooked rice
- 1 tablespoon fish liver oil
- 1,000 mg taurine
- 1 teaspoon eggshell powder

Directions:

1. Grind the turkey meat and innards, or pulverize in a food processor.

2. Mix in the carrot or pumpkin and rice.

3. Add in the vegetable and rice mix, along with fish liver oil, taurine, and eggshell powder.

Recipe 28: Ground meat meal

If you do not want to invest in a grinder, you can always purchase ground meat from your local grocer and add finely chopped organ meats and innards to it.

Ingredients:

- 3 cups ground meat (beef, chicken, or turkey)
- 1 cup organ meat (Ask your butcher for "leftovers": liver, heart, or kidney.)
- 1 cup cooked rolled oats
- ¼ cup each cooked green beans and carrots
- 1 tablespoon fish liver oil
- 1 teaspoon eggshell powder

Directions:

1. Finely chop or use a food processor to process the innards and organ meats until they are mushy.

2. Mix the processed meats thoroughly with ground meats.

3. Add in oats, vegetables, oil, and eggshell powder.

Complete Meals

The following recipes will provide enough food for several meals. For convenience, you can divide the completed recipes into single servings of approximately ½ cup of cooked foods or 2 heaping tablespoons of the raw recipes and freeze in small, resealable plastic bags. Move into refrigerator as needed.

Recipe 29: Turkey hash

Ingredients:

- 3 tablespoons fat (any animal source)
- 1 ½ pounds ground turkey
- 1 cup turkey gravy (or chicken gravy, if you cannot find turkey gravy)
- 2 cups cubed peeled and cooked
- 1 tablespoon fresh, chopped parsley
- 1 teaspoon eggshell powder
- 1,000 mg taurine

Directions:

1. Melt the fat in a skillet.
2. Add turkey and potatoes, stirring to mix well.
3. Cook for 3 to 4 minutes, applying pressure to mash down with a spatula until a "cake" is formed.
4. Lower the heat to medium.
5. Pour on the gravy or cream.
6. Sprinkle with parsley, stir in the eggshells and taurine, and then cook for another 5 minutes.

Recipe 30: Turkey-tuna surprise

Ingredients:

- 1 pound ground turkey
- 1 cup carrots, chopped
- 1 can tuna
- 1 cup cooked rice
- 1 teaspoon eggshell powder
- 1,000 mg taurine

Directions:

1. Brown turkey in a frying pan. Allow to cool.

2. Blanch carrots, cooking just until barely done.

3. Empty tuna into mixing bowl.

4. Mash cooked carrots into tuna.

5. Stir in the rice and turkey.

6. Add in eggshell powder and taurine.

Recipe 31: Turkey with potatoes and peas

Ingredients:

- 1 pound turkey breasts
- ½ pound turkey thighs
- 1 to 3 tablespoons chicken fat or fish liver oil
- 1 cup cooked, cubed potatoes
- ¼ cup frozen peas, thawed
- 100 mg taurine
- ¾ teaspoon eggshell powder

Directions:

1. Mince all turkey meat.

2. Cook turkey in fat until done.

3. Stir in potatoes and peas.

4. Continue cooking until peas are mushy.

5. Remove from heat, and stir in the taurine and eggshell powder.

Recipe 32: Turkey with sweet potatoes and rice

Ingredients:

- 1 ½ pounds ground turkey, mixed light and dark meat
- 1 to 3 tablespoons chicken fat or fish liver oil
- 1 sweet potato
- ½ cup cooked rice
- 100 mg taurine
- ¾ teaspoon eggshell powder

Directions:

1. Bake sweet potato in 400° F oven until done (about 1 hour)
2. Meanwhile, sauté turkey in chicken fat until done.
3. Remove potato from oven, slice open, and mash with a potato masher until no chunks remain.
4. Place pulp of sweet potato into a bowl. Mix in the rice and ground turkey.
5. Sprinkle in the taurine and eggshell powder.

Recipe 33: Any day trout casserole

Ingredients:

- 1 pound trout
- ½ cup whole oats
- 1 egg
- 100 mg taurine
- ¾ teaspoon eggshell powder

Directions:

1. Preheat oven to 400° F.

2. In a blender or food processor, pulverize the oats until are meal and crumbly.

3. Finely chop the trout.

4. Scramble the egg and pour into a large, resealable plastic bag.

5. Dump the trout and pulverized oats into the bag.

6. Seal bag and shake, ensuring trout, egg, and oat mixture is evenly mixed and distributed.

7. Pour contents into casserole dish.

8. Bake for 25 minutes.

9. Sprinkle eggshell powder and taurine on top before storing.

Recipe 34: Tuna and rice

Ingredients:
- 3 tablespoons fat
- 2 cups cooked rice
- 7-ounce can tuna
- ¼ cup carrots
- ¼ cup celery
- 100 mg taurine
- 1 teaspoon eggshells

Directions:
1. Melt the fat. Add the carrots and celery and cook over medium heat until soft.
2. Stir in tuna and rice, and heat through.
3. Add in the taurine and eggshell powder.

Recipe 35: Scrambled eggs

No specific amounts of eggs are given here, as you may just want to make an egg for your kitty while you whisk one up for the human members of the family, though you can hold off on putting the taurine and eggshell powder onto the human's food.

Ingredients:
- Eggs
- Water
- 1,000 mg taurine per egg
- ½ teaspoon eggshell powder per egg

Directions
1. Crack the eggs into a bowl.
2. Add 1 teaspoon water for each egg, and whisk together with the taurine.
3. Spray skillet with non-stick cooking spray, and set over low heat.
4. Pour in egg mixture and cook, stirring constantly until desired doneness.
5. Sprinkle eggshell powder over cooked eggs.

Recipe 36 & 37: Scrambled Egg Varieties

Scrambled Eggs with Lox

1. Fry ½ slice lox, chopped fine, per egg in pan before adding egg mixture.
2. Stir all together to cook.

Scrambled Eggs with Chicken Livers

1. You will not need to add the taurine if using chicken livers.
2. Use 1 chicken liver per 2 eggs.
3. Mince liver.
4. Fry in pan before adding egg mixture.

Recipe 38: Sardines in a snap

Ingredients:

- 2 cans sardines in oil
- ¼ cup chopped fresh parsley
- ⅔ cup cooked rice
- 1 egg, hard-boiled
- 2 chicken livers
- 1 teaspoon eggshell powder

Directions:

1. Boil chicken livers for 15 minutes.
2. Allow cooling.
3. Place sardines, rice, livers, parsley, egg, and eggshells in food processor, and pulse to blend.
4. Each time you serve this to your cat, sprinkle ½ teaspoon eggshell powder over it.

Recipe 39: Turkey mix

Ingredients:

- 1 cup cooked turkey meat
- 1 egg, hard-boiled
- ½ cup cooked carrots
- ½ cup chicken broth
- 1 cup cooked rice
- 250 mg taurine
- 1 tablespoon eggshell powder

Directions:

1. Chop and mince turkey, egg, and carrots, alternately pulverize in a food processor, but do not allow it to liquefy.
2. Stir in rice, broth, taurine, and eggshell powder, mixing well.

Recipe 40: Chicken with rice and greens

Ingredients:

- 1 pound chicken breasts
- ½ pound chicken thighs
- 1 to 3 tablespoons chicken fat or fish liver oil
- 1 cup cooked rice
- ¼ cup chopped greens (collard, Swiss chard or your cat's favorite)
- 100 mg taurine
- ¾ teaspoon eggshell powder

Directions:

1. Mince or pulverize chicken in a food processor.
2. Cook chicken in a skillet in the fat until done.
3. Stir in rice and greens.
4. Continue cooking until greens are soft.
5. Remove from heat and stir in the taurine and eggshell powder.

Recipe 41: Rabbit with potatoes and carrots

Ingredients:

- 1 whole rabbit
- 1+ cup chicken broth
- 1 cup cooked, cubed potatoes
- ¼ cup shredded carrots
- 100 mg taurine
- ¾ teaspoon eggshell powder

Directions:

1. Chop rabbit into small, kitty-bite-sized pieces.
2. Braise rabbit in the broth, adding broth as it evaporates to keep rabbit covered.
3. Stir in potatoes and carrots.
4. Continue cooking until carrots are soft.
5. Remove from heat, and stir in the taurine and eggshell powder.

Recipe 42: Poached salmon

Ingredients:

- 6 pounds whole salmon
- 4 carrots, sliced
- 6 quarts water
- 1 cup celery, chopped
- 1 teaspoon eggshells
- 1,000 mg taurine

Directions:

1. If you do not have a fish poacher, use a roasting pan with a lid and a rack that will hold the fish.

2. Combine water and vegetables in pan.

3. Bring to a boil, reduce heat, and simmer 15 minutes.

4. Lay fish on rack and add more water if needed to cover.

5. Replace lid and simmer 25 to 30 minutes or until meat is no longer deep pink around the backbone.

6. Remove pan from heat, but let fish remain in broth up to 45 minutes.

7. Remove fish and vegetables; finely dice so that your cat can comfortably eat it.

8. Reserve broth for other recipes.

Recipe 43: Boiled chicken with oats and celery

Ingredients:

- 1 whole chicken with innards
- 4 celery stalks, chopped
- 6 quarts water
- 1 cup cooked, whole oats
- 1 teaspoon eggshells
- 1,000 mg taurine

Directions:

1. Cut chicken into quarters.

2. Place chicken parts and innards along with celery in a pot, and cover with water.

3. Bring to a boil, reduce heat, and simmer 30 minutes.

4. Drain chicken and celery, reserving liquid.

5. When chicken is cool to the touch, remove all meat from the bone.

6. Process chicken meat and celery in a food blender

7. Pour cooked oats into a large bowl; add the chicken meat and celery. Stir well.

8. Add in eggshells and taurine.

Recipe 44: Baked mackerel and potatoes

Ingredients:

- 3 potatoes, peeled or diced
- 2 ½ pounds mackerel fillets
- 1 teaspoon eggshells
- 1,000 mg taurine

Directions:

1. Preheat oven to 400° F.

2. Boil potatoes for 5 minutes (Note: They will not be done.).

3. Drain potatoes and spread on the bottom of a baking sheet sprayed with non-stick spray.

4. Place fish over the potatoes, and bake for 20 minutes.

Recipe 45: Rabbit stew, almost Brunswick style

Ingredients:

- 4 to 6 pounds chopped rabbit
- 3 white peeled potatoes
- 1 cup green beans
- 1 teaspoon eggshell powder
- 1,000 mg taurine

Directions:

1. Place rabbit in pot. and cover with water.

2. Bring to a boil, and simmer 40 minutes.

3. While rabbit is boiling, chop the vegetables into 1-inch pieces.

4. Remove rabbit from broth, and allow cooling enough to handle.

5. Place vegetables into broth, and boil gently for 30 minutes.

6. Mince rabbit, and keep aside until the 30 minutes for the vegetables cooking are up.

7. Return rabbit to the pot, and simmer for another 10 minutes; add the taurine and eggshell powder.

Recipe 46: Braised rabbit

Ingredients:

- 4 tablespoons fat
- 2 rabbits, cut into chunks
- 2 cups chicken broth
- 1 cup chopped carrots
- 1 teaspoon eggshells
- 1,000 mg taurine

Directions:

1. Heat the fat in a heavy skillet.

2. Add rabbit pieces, and brown on all sides.

3. Pour in broth.

4. Cover, and simmer for 20 to 25 minutes, or until when speared, the juices run clear.

5. Add in the taurine and eggshell powder.

Recipe 47: Rabbit and veggies

Ingredients:

- 2 rabbits
- ½ cup cooked, finely chopped carrots
- ½ cup peas
- ½ cup cooked rice, cooked in broth (any kind)
- 1 tablespoon fish liver oil
- 1 teaspoon eggshells
- 1,000 mg taurine

Directions:

1. Cut rabbit into small chunks. Boil for 20 minutes, or until done.
2. Drain, and mince the rabbit meat.
3. Stir together all ingredients, mixing well.

Recipe 48: Oats and beef loaf

Ingredients:

- 2 pounds full-fat ground beef
- 1 cup chopped carrots
- 4 cups rolled oats
- ¼ cup ground, dried kelp (found in the Asian aisle at your supermarket)
- 2 eggs
- 1,000 mg taurine
- 1 teaspoon eggshell powder

Directions:

1. Preheat oven to 345° F.
2. Cook oats according to package directions.
3. In large bowl, combine beef, carrots, eggs, and kelp.
4. Pour into loaf pan.
5. Bake for 45 minutes.
6. Divide into serving-size chunks.
7. Sprinkle all with taurine and eggshell powder.

Recipe 49: Tuna and rice soup

Ingredients:

- 1 pound tuna steak, chopped
- 1 tablespoon fish oil
- 2 cups water (or fish broth)
- 1 cup rice
- 2 stalks celery, cubed
- 1,000 mg taurine
- 1 teaspoon eggshell powder

Directions:

1. Preheat oven to 345° F.
2. Lightly brown the tuna in the oil in a skillet.
3. Place the tuna, water (or broth), celery, and rice in a stockpot.
4. Bring to a boil, reduce heat, and simmer for 25 minutes.
5. Stir in the taurine and the eggshell powder.

Recipe 50: Steak and potato stew

Ingredients:

- 1 pound beef (alternately, you may use cooked leftovers, cubed)
- 3 cups peeled, white potatoes
- 2 cups beef broth
- 1 tablespoon chopped barley or wheatgrass
- ½ cup cooked green beans
- 1 teaspoon eggshell powder
- 1,000 mg taurine

Directions:

1. Broil beef, being careful not to char. Allow to cool, and set aside.
2. Chop potatoes. Place potatoes in pot and cover with beef broth, adding in water, if necessary, to completely cover them.
3. Bring to boil, reduce heat, and simmer for 15 minutes.
4. Add in the green beans, and cook an additional 3 to 5 minutes or until potatoes easily break apart when touched with a fork.
5. Drain potatoes and beans.
6. Cube beef.
7. Pulverize beef, potatoes, and green beans in a food processor.
8. Stir in chopped grass, eggshell powder, and taurine.

Recipe 51: Extra-moist beef and oats

Ingredients:

- 1 pound beef, any cut, cubed
- 2 cups beef broth
- ½ cup rolled oats
- ½ cup each chopped carrots and celery
- 1 teaspoon eggshell powder
- 1,000 mg taurine

Directions:

1. Cook beef in simmering broth for 20 minutes, or until done.
2. Add oats, carrots, and celery; bring to boil (adding water, if necessary, to keep all covered).
3. Reduce heat to simmer. Cover, and allow to cook until oats are done (7 to 12 minutes).
4. Strain, reserving water.
5. Pour beef, oats, and vegetables into food processor, and pulverize until well mixed, and all meat is shredded.
6. Mix in grass, eggshell, and taurine.
7. Add reserved water if your cat likes even more moisture.

Recipe 52: Cornish game hen balls

Ingredients:

- 1 ½ pound Cornish game hen
- 2 cups cooked rice
- 2 eggs
- ½ cup steamed or par-boiled carrots
- 1 teaspoon eggshell powder
- 1,000 mg taurine

Directions:

1. Boil whole Cornish game hen until meat falls off the bone easily.

2. Allow hen to cool until you can comfortably handle it with your hands.

3. Remove all the meat from the carcass, and discard all of the bones.

4. Scramble eggs in a non-stick pan, or lightly coat the pan with non-stick spray.

5. In a food processor, pulverize all ingredients.

6. Form into small, kitty-bite-sized balls.

Recipe 53: Chicken and vegetable stew

Ingredients:

- 1 small chicken, about 3 pounds
- ½ cup carrots, chopped
- Innards from a chicken: gizzards, liver, and heart
- ½ cup celery, chopped
- ½ cup peas
- 1 teaspoon eggshell powder
- 1,000 mg taurine

Directions:

1. Cut the chicken into quarters.

2. Boil chicken, cut chicken pieces and the insides until meat falls off the bone (approximately 25 minutes).

3. Remove chicken, reserving the broth.

4. Strip the chicken bones of all meat and skin. Discard all of the bones.

5. Finely chop all the chicken meat; alternately, process in a food processor.

6. Return meat to broth, stir in vegetables, and simmer until vegetables are tender.

7. Drain, but not completely, so that you keep the food matter moist.

8. Sprinkle with taurine and eggshell powder, and stir in.

Just Meat

These recipes do not call for any eggshell powder or taurine. Those nutrients will need to be added when the foods are chopped up and served to your kitty. At that time, add 250 mg taurine and ½ teaspoon eggshell powder. Adding the rice or vegetables from the Supplement and Accompaniment Recipe Section will make these complete meals.

Recipe 54: Easy baked fresh tuna

Ingredients:

- 1 ¾ pounds fresh tuna steaks
- Fish liver oil

Directions:

1. Preheat oven to 425° F.
2. Rub tuna steaks with oil.
3. Place in oven and bake for 12 to 15 minutes, depending on how thick the tuna is.

Recipe 55: Roasted guinea fowl

Game fowl, because of its wild nature, generally has less fat and will be a tougher kind of meat. Younger birds are tenderer, if you know you have an older bird, increasing the fat will make it easier for your tabby to chew as well as making it tastier.

Ingredients:

- 2 guinea fowl
- ¼ pound chicken or beef fat

Directions:

1. Preheat oven to 350° F.
2. Place on roasting pan, and baste the breasts with fat.
3. Roast for 45 to 60 minutes, basting every 15 to 20 with the drippings to keep moist.

Recipe 56: Broiled quail

Ingredients:

- 2 quail
- 4 tablespoons fat, melted to liquid form

Directions:

1. Preheat broiler.
2. Rinse quail and pat dry.
3. Split each quail down the center, breaking into halves.
4. Brush the quail with the melted fat, and place, skin side down, on a broiler pan about 5 inches below heat source.
5. Broil 5 minutes on each side, basting frequently to prevent drying out.

Recipe 57: Finicky eaters meal

Ingredients:

- 1 cup boiled chicken
- ¼ cup steamed broccoli
- ¼ cup steamed, shredded carrots
- Chicken broth

Directions:

1. Mix ingredients together with enough broth to keep together.
2. Cook for 10 to 15 minutes on medium setting.
3. Let cool for 5 to 10 minutes before serving.

Note: This recipe can also be used with fish as a replacement. You can also add in rice or vegetables to vary the recipe.

Recipe 58: Braised steak

Broiling steak is not good for cuts that are not loaded with fat. The tougher cuts of meat will be moister if boiled or braised.

Ingredients:

- 1 pound steak — flank or brisket
- 3 tablespoons melted chicken fat
- 2 cups beef broth
- ¼ cup chopped parsley

Directions:

1. Preheat oven to 400° F.
2. Cube the steak, and quickly brown it in the chicken fat.
3. Place steak in baking pan, and pour over the broth.
4. Cover the baking pan with foil
5. Bake in oven for 1 hour.

Recipe 59: Baked chicken

Ingredients:

- 1 whole chicken
- ¼ pound melted chicken fat

Directions:

1. Preheat oven to 375° F.
2. Rinse chicken, and pat dry.
3. Place chicken on roasting rack, breast side up.
4. With basting brush, baste chicken with melted fat.
5. Bake in the oven for 15 minutes per pound of chicken, rebasting with fat and drippings every 14 minutes.
6. When chicken is done, remove, and allow to cool.
7. Once cool to touch, strip bones of all meat.
8. Mince meat well.

Recipe 60: Turkey morsels

Ingredients:

- 1 ½ pounds turkey meat, any variety
- ¼ pound melted chicken fat

Directions:

1. Finely chop turkey meat, or grind in a meat grinder.
2. Over low heat, sauté the turkey meat in the fat until done, and meat is crumbly.

Recipe 61: Everyday beef

Ingredients:

- 1 ½ pounds beef — flank steak or brisket
- 2 cups beef broth

Directions:

1. Chop the beef into small, kitty-bite-sized pieces.
2. Place in stockpot, and cover with broth.
3. Bring to a boil, then simmer for 30 minutes.
4. When done, drain, but only a little — you want the meat to remain moist, but not in a soup-like state.

Recipe 62: Duck legs

Duck legs are not the easiest meat source to find, but if you ask your butcher, he or she will be able to supply you with as many as your cat would like.

Ingredients:

- 6 duck legs
- 2 tablespoons chicken fat
- 1 cup chicken broth

Directions:

1. Preheat oven to 425° F.
2. Melt the fat in a skillet over medium heat.
3. Set duck legs into the fat, skin side down.
4. Cook until browned, about 8 minutes.
5. Turn over, and brown the other side for about 3 minutes.
6. Remove from heat, and place in roasting pan; cover with foil.
7. Cover with the broth, and bake for 1 hour 15 minutes.
8. Lift off the foil, and turn the legs over.
9. Continue roasting until the legs are tender when poked with a fork.

Recipe 63: Braised lamb

Ingredients:

- 6 lamb shoulder chop steaks
- 2 tablespoons chicken fat
- 1 cup chicken broth

Directions:

1. Preheat oven to 325° F.
2. Melt the chicken fat in a heavy skillet on top of stove.
3. Brown the lamb chops in the fat.
4. Place in a Dutch oven, and pour in the broth (adding more if necessary to cover the meat).
5. Place lid on Dutch oven, and bake for 1 ½ hours.
6. Remove meat, and allow to cool.
7. Mince, or pulverize in a food processor, adding more broth if necessary to keep the meat moist.

Treats & Meals for Dairy Tolerant Cats

If you know that your cat is dairy tolerant, you can try creating the following recipes for him or her. Otherwise, you may wish to avoid this section entirely.

Recipe 64: Summertime cottage cheese treat

Ingredients:

- 8 ounces cottage cheese

Directions:

1. Partially fill disposable muffin cups with cottage cheese.
2. Place on baking sheet, and freeze overnight.
3. The next morning, scoop off the liquid that separated and pooled in the top of each muffin cup. Discard.
4. Keep remainder in muffin cups in the freezer section of your refrigerator until ready to give to your cat. He or she may really appreciate one of these after a hot time in the sun.

Recipe 65: Tuna balls snacks

Ingredients:

- 1 cup pulverized whole oats
- 1 cup non-fat powdered milk
- 1 can tuna, packed in oil
- ¼ cup water
- 1 egg

Directions:

1. Preheat oven to 350° F.

2. Empty the can of tuna into a mixing bowl (you will want both the oil and the fish).

3. Mash the tuna with a fork, breaking it up as much as you can.

4. Add in the pulverized whole oats and powdered milk.

5. Scramble the egg, and mix in the water.

6. Pour the egg/water mixture into the tuna, oats, and milk.

7. Mix all together.

8. Roll into balls, and bake on cookie sheet sprayed with non-stick spray for 10 minutes.

Recipe 66: Parmesan-sprinkled chicken tenders

Ingredients:

- 1 pound chicken breasts
- 3 tablespoons melted chicken fat or other safe oil
- ¼ cup grated Parmesan

Directions:

1. Preheat oven to 375° F.

2. Cut chicken breasts into long, thin strips.

3. Place in baking pan, and baste with fat.

4. Bake for 10 minutes, basting frequently at least twice with fat or drippings.

5. Sprinkle top with Parmesan, and continue baking until the cheese melts.

Recipe 67: Oaty catnip cookies

Ingredients:

- 1 cup pulverized whole oats
- ¼ cup rice or oat flour
- 1 teaspoon chopped catnip
- 1 egg
- ⅓ cup whole milk
- 2 tablespoons rice bran
- ⅓ cup powdered milk
- Fish liver oil as needed

Directions:

1. Preheat oven to 350° F.

2. Combine all dry ingredients in a mixing bowl. Set aside.

3. In another large bowl, combine egg and milk.

4. Add in the dry ingredients, stirring while adding until all are blended evenly together.

5. If more liquid is needed, add in fish liver oil.

6. When dough forms, roll it out onto a board dusted with rice flower.

7. Use small cookie cutters, or cut into ¼-inch squares.

8. Bake on baking sheet covered with non-stick spray for 12 to 15 minutes.

Recipe 68: Oaty tuna treats

Ingredients:

- 1 can tuna packed in oil
- ½ cup rice flour
- ½ cup powdered milk
- ½ cup crushed rolled oats
- 1 tablespoon fish liver oil
- 1 egg
- ¼ cup chicken broth if needed

Directions:

1. Preheat oven to 350° F.
2. In a mixing bowl, break tuna up with a fork.
3. In separate, larger bowl, mix rice flour, powdered milk, and crushed oats.
4. Beat egg.
5. Mix egg, fish liver oil, and tuna into dry ingredients, adding in broth if needed, until the consistency is sticky.
6. Knead with hands on rice-floured board until dough is workable.
7. Form into small balls, and place onto a cookie sheet sprayed with non-stick spray.
8. Bake for 12 to 15 minutes.

Recipe 69: Crab cookies

Ingredients:

- ½ cup whole milk
- 4 crab sticks (real — do not use artificial crab, which often contains artificial food coloring)
- 1 egg
- ½ cup crushed rolled oats

Directions:

1. Preheat oven to 350° F.
2. Shred the crab with a fork, or pulverize it in a food processor.
3. Mix all ingredients until they hold together enough to flatten and cut into squares, or use cookie cutters to cut small shapes.
4. Bake for 15 minutes or until golden brown.

Recipe 70: Chicken meatballs

Ingredients:

- 1 ½ pounds ground chicken, a mix of both light and dark meats
- 1 cup cooked rice or whole oats, whichever your cat prefers
- ¼ cup shredded carrots
- 1 egg
- ¼ cup grated Parmesan cheese
- 1 tablespoon melted chicken fat
- 1,000 mg taurine

Directions:

1. Preheat oven to 375° F.
2. Mix chicken together with the rice or oats, carrots, egg, and cheese.
3. Form small balls of the meat mixture.
4. Place on broil pan, and bake in oven for 30 minutes.
5. Baste with chicken fat, and sprinkle with taurine (the chicken fat will help it stick).

Recipe 71: Turkey hash with cottage cheese

Ingredients:

- 1 ½ pounds turkey legs and thighs on bone
- 2 cups cooked rice
- 1 cup cottage cheese
- 1 egg, hard-boiled
- 6 tablespoons chopped greens of your choice
- 1,000 mg taurine

Directions:

1. In a large pot, boil turkey until the meat easily comes off of the bone.
2. Allow turkey to cool so that you can handle it comfortably.
3. Separate turkey meat from bone.
4. Combine turkey, rice, cottage cheese, egg, greens, and taurine in a food processor, and pulse until well blended.

Recipe 72: Crepes

At first glance, crepes may seem like a labor-intensive food to make for your cat, but they freeze extremely well, in that they do not lose any flavor or texture in the freezing process as some foods can. Make a large batch, and stack them with layers of foil between each one for easy retrieval.

Ingredients:

- 2 eggs
- 1 cup rice flour
- 1 cup milk
- 2 tablespoons fat, melted

Directions:

1. Beat eggs thoroughly.

2. Add milk, salt, rice flour, and fat.

3. Let stand for at least 30 minutes.

4. Heat a small frying pan, a 7-inch skillet will do, over medium heat, and spray with non-stick spray.

5. Pour in egg mixture, tilting the pan so the bottom is coated evenly with the eggs, as thin as you can get it.

6. Cook until the bottom is lightly browned, and the edges lift easily with a spatula.

7. Flip, and cook for a few minutes more.

8. Slide off pan, and make another until all egg mixture is used.

9. As you feed them to your kitty, sprinkle with a serving of taurine (250 mg).

Recipe 73: Turkey crepes

Ingredients:

- 4 tablespoons fat
- 2 egg yolks, beaten
- ¼ cup rice flour
- 2 cups diced, cooked turkey
- 1 ½ cups heavy cream, reserve ½ cup
- ¾ cup chicken broth
- 12 7-inch crepes, (recipe above)
- ¼ cup water
- 1,000 mg taurine

Directions:

1. Preheat oven to 350° F.
2. Melt the fat in skillet on stove top.
3. Add rice flour, and then slowly pour in 1 cup cream, stirring constantly.
4. Add broth and water, and stir over medium heat until thick.
5. Cool for 5 minutes.
6. Stir 3 tablespoons of cooled sauce into the yolks, and then add in the turkey to create filling.
7. Fill each crepe with 3 tablespoons of filling.
8. Roll, and place, seam side down, in a baking dish.
9. Add remaining cream to sauce, and spread over crepes.
10. Bake for 25 minutes.
11. Sprinkle with taurine when done.

Recipe 74: Chicken livers and cheese

Ingredients:

- 4 chicken livers
- ¼ cup rolled oats
- ⅔ cup cottage cheese
- 2 tablespoons chicken fat
- 1 egg, hard-boiled
- 1,000 mg taurine

Directions:

1. Boil chicken livers for 15 minutes.

2. Drain, and allow cooling.

3. Combine all ingredients into a food processor; pulse to blend.

Recipe 75: Chicken and rice "casserole"

Ingredients:

- 1 small chicken, about 3 pounds
- 1 cup rice
- ½ cup cooked celery
- 2 cups chicken broth
- ½ cup Parmesan cheese
- 1,000 mg taurine

Directions:

1. Cut the chicken into quarters.

2. In a large pot of boiling water, cook chicken until the meat falls off the bone.

3. Allow chicken to cool thoroughly.

4. Separate meat from the bones of the chicken, stripping the carcass clean.

5. Discard the bones.

6. Cook rice and celery in broth until rice is done.

7. Combine chicken, rice, carrots, Parmesan, and taurine, and mix well.

Recipe 76: Almost chicken divan

Ingredients:

- 1 cup cooked, chopped broccoli
- 2 cups chicken gravy
- 2 cups chopped, cooked chicken
- ½ cup Parmesan cheese
- 1,000 mg taurine

Directions:

1. Preheat oven to 375° F.
2. Spray a baking dish with non-stick spray.
3. Spread broccoli on bottom of dish.
4. Place chicken over broccoli.
5. Spoon gravy over all, and sprinkle with the cheese.
6. Bake 15 to 20 minutes until heated all the way through, and cheese begins to melt.

Recipe 77: Not-quite chicken Parmesan

Ingredients:

- 1 small, whole chicken
- ½ cup cooked rolled oats
- ½ cup chicken broth
- ½ cup Parmesan cheese
- 1 teaspoon fish liver oil
- 1,000 mg taurine

Directions:

1. Cut the chicken into quarters.
2. In a large pot, boil the chicken until the meat easily falls off the bone.
3. Allow chicken to cool thoroughly.
4. Remove all meat and skin from chicken, and discard the carcass.
5. Mince chicken meat; alternately, pulverize it in a food processor.
6. Stir together meat, oats, broth, and Parmesan cheese.
7. Mix in fish liver oil and taurine.

Recipe 78: Not your mother's meatloaf

Ingredients:

- 1 ½ pounds ground meat
- 2 cups cooked rice
- 2 eggs
- ½ cup steamed or par-boiled carrots
- ¼ cup shredded cheddar cheese
- 1 teaspoon eggshell powder
- 1,000 mg taurine

Directions:

1. Preheat oven to 375° F.
2. Mix meat, rice, eggs, and carrots together.
3. Press into loaf pan, and place in oven.
4. Bake for 45 minutes.
5. Sprinkle cheese over the top.
6. Return to oven, and bake until cheese is melted.

Recipe 79: Beef and potatoes au gratin-style

Ingredients:

- 1 pound high-fat ground beef
- 3 cups peeled, cooked potatoes
- ½ cup heavy cream
- 2 tablespoons cooked broccoli
- ¼ cup grated Parmesan cheese
- 2 tablespoons cooked parsley
- 1000 mg taurine

Directions:

1. Preheat oven to 350° F.

2. Fry ground beef until browned, and drain.

3. In casserole dish, layer beef, potatoes, and vegetables.

4. Pour cream over the top of it all.

5. Cover with the grated Parmesan cheese.

6. Bake for 15 minutes or until cheese begins to melt.

7. Sprinkle taurine on top.

Recipe 80: Egg and mackerel casserole

Ingredients:

- 2 eggs
- 1 ½ cups whole milk
- ½ cup raw vegetables
- 2 cans mackerel
- 1 cup cooked rice
- 1,000 mg taurine
- 1 tablespoon fish liver oil

Directions:

1. Preheat oven to 350° F.

2. Blend together eggs and milk.

3. Add in the rice.

4. Shred or process vegetables in food processor until pulverized; mix in with eggs, milk, and rice.

5. Shred mackerel with a fork, or pulverize in food processor.

6. Stir mackerel, the oil from the mackerel cans, and the extra fish-liver oil into vegetables, egg mix.

7. Bake mixture in oven for 20 minutes.

8. Sprinkle top evenly with taurine.

Meals to Share

You may have thought a few of the previously mentioned meals would be nice to have for yourself. Likewise, you can always take part of your meals and share them with your favorite feline. For example, you can easily share your leisurely weekend brunch with your favorite furry friend if you are careful of what you put in your omelet. And you can include that same feline in on the special holiday fare. Why should they be left out of some of our most special occasions? Here are just a few recipes to get you started.

Recipe 81: Stuffed omelet

Ingredients:

- 3 eggs
- 2 tablespoons drained and diced zucchini, broccoli, or carrots
- 1 tablespoon finely chopped fresh parsley
- 1 tablespoon finely grated Parmesan cheese

Directions:

1. Stir eggs in a bowl until well blended.
2. Pour the eggs into a preheated sauté pan, and cook just long enough for the bottom to become solid.
3. Add in vegetables, parsley, and cheese.
4. Using a spatula, fold one side of the egg over onto itself.
5. Allow to cook for 30 seconds. Flip entire egg over, and cook another 30 seconds.
6. Slide egg out onto plate, and sprinkle with taurine on the part set aside for the cat.

Recipe 82: Chicken fried rice

Ingredients:

- 1 pound chicken, cubed
- 2 tablespoons chicken fat
- 2 tablespoons diced zucchini, broccoli, or carrots
- 1 egg
- 1 cup cooked rice
- 1 teaspoon eggshell powder
- 1,000 mg taurine

Directions:

1. Crack egg, and mix it well, set aside.

2. Sauté chicken in fat.

3. Add in the vegetables, and cook one minute.

4. Add in the rice; cook another minute, constantly stirring.

5. Pour in the egg, and cook, stirring non-stop until egg is done.

6. Add in the eggshell powder and the taurine.

Recipe 83: Thanksgiving turkey

Ingredients:

- 1 pound ground turkey (both light and dark meat)
- 1 of each: turkey heart, liver, and gizzard
- 1 tablespoon canned pumpkin (not pumpkin pie filling)
- 1 tablespoon cooked mashed potatoes (with no butter or milk, just potatoes, please)
- ¾ teaspoon eggshell powder

Directions:

1. Brown the ground turkey in a skillet.

2. Stew the heart, liver, and gizzard in simmering water for 20 minutes, and then drain.

3. Finely chop and dice organ meats, add to ground turkey.

4. Stir in pumpkin, potatoes, and eggshell powder.

Recipe 84: Spring leg of lamb steaks

Ingredients:

- 4 lamb steaks (cut from a leg)
- 2 tablespoons melted chicken fat
- 2 tablespoons fresh mint
- 1 tablespoon cooked mashed potatoes (with no butter or milk, just potatoes, please)
- ¾ teaspoon eggshell powder
- 1,000 mg taurine

Directions:

1. Rub the melted fat over the lamb steaks. .

2. Place on broiler pan, and broil, about 6 inches away from the heat source for about 6 minutes.

3. Turn lamb steaks over, brush other side with the fat, and return to broiler for another 6 minutes.

4. Allow to cool.

5. Chop, and place into a food processor along with the mint and potatoes. Process until mealy.

6. Stir in eggshell powder.

Recipes for Special Health Concerns

As discussed in Chapter 6, diet plays several roles in the health of your cat. The foods you feed him or her can both impact health and help ease specific conditions. The following recipes are geared toward particular physiological issues from which your cat may be suffering. However, before offering your cat any food for a specific condition, be sure to discuss what you intend to do with your veterinarian. Your cat may be in a category all by itself, and what might help another cat in similar distress, could possibly make yours worse.

Recipe 85: Food for food allergies

Sometimes a cat will suffer from gastrointestinal issues or other health conditions as a direct result of food allergies or intolerances. Should you suspect food allergies with your tabby, feeding a diet based on lamb and rice for a couple of weeks should clear up the symptoms, as they are the least allergenic foods. Once your cat seems to have recovered, you can start to reintroduce foods one at a time to see which are the offending foods. You may also want to use distilled water during the allergen-free time, as occasionally, municipal waters have compounds in them that can cause allergic reactions. The following is a simple, yet safe, allergen-free meal.

Ingredients:
- 1 pound lamb
- ½ cup rice
- 1 teaspoon powdered eggshell
- 1,000 mg taurine

Directions:
1. Do not remove fat from lamb.
2. Cube the lamb and cook (either braising or roasting works well).
3. Meanwhile, cook the rice with distilled water.
4. Pulverize the cooked lamb in a food processor.

5. Mix lamb and rice thoroughly, stirring in the eggshell and taurine when cool enough to handle.

Recipe 86: Tummy trouble tea

Sometimes an upset stomach just happens. If you suspect your cat is suffering from nausea or indigestion, keep slippery elm bark on hand to whip up this mixture. The bulk powder is usually quite easy to find in your local health-food store. If you cannot locate any, you can buy it in capsule form. You can then empty the capsules to mix into the water. Be sure to check the grams of the capsule, as you may need to adjust the amount. One-fourth tablespoon of slipper elm bark usually weighs 1.2 grams, and the capsules may not as it is ground more finely inside the capsule. You may give your cat 3 to 5 cc of this tea from a medicine dropper up to three times a day to help ease symptoms (medicine droppers from your local pharmacy will have the cc, or cubic centimeter, marks notated on them). Refrain from giving it to him or her at mealtime or along with another medicine.

Ingredients:
- ½ teaspoon slipper elm bark bulk powder
- 2 tablespoons boiled water

Directions:
1. Place the powder in a small glass ramekin (an empty baby jar will do, too).
2. Pour the hot water in, and mix gently. Cover, but not air tight, and allow to cool.
3. When cool mix thoroughly again.

Recipe 87: Easy-on-the-stomach chicken and rice

Ingredients:

- 1 pound chicken, cubed.
- 1 cup cooked rice
- ¼ cup each canned pumpkin and steamed, chopped green beans
- Chicken broth
- 1 teaspoon eggshell powder
- 1,000 mg taurine

Directions:

1. Cover chicken with broth, and boil until done (about 20 minutes).
2. Drain, but if cubes are too large for your cat to easily chew, pulverize chicken in a food processor.
3. Stir in rice, vegetables, eggshell powder, and taurine.

Recipe 88: Bladder and kidney-friendly beef

Cats suffering with bladder and kidney problems sometimes need to increase their water intake to help prevent stones from forming in their urine. At other times, cats will need to lower their protein intake.

Note: This recipe includes salt to encourage water drinking, and not all cats should be eating salt. It is imperative you speak with the veterinarian who is treating your cat for bladder or kidney problems before you include salt in your cat's diet.

Ingredients:
- 2 pounds ground beef
- ¼ pound beef liver
- 2 cups cooked rice
- 1 teaspoon fish liver oil
- 1 teaspoon salt
- 2 tablespoons chopped kale
- 1 teaspoon eggshell powder

Directions:
1. Finely chop up beef liver.
2. Combine liver with ground beef, and brown in a frying pan.
3. Mix cooked rice, fish liver oil, salt, and kale into pan.
4. Continue cooking until kale is tender.
5. Stir in eggshell powder.

Recipe 89: Lower protein for better kidneys

Ingredients:

- ½ pound cooked beef or chicken liver
- 2 eggs, hard boiled
- 3 cups cooked rice
- 1 tablespoon fish liver oil
- 1 teaspoon eggshell powder

Directions:

1. Mince liver, and fry in a non-stick pan.
2. Finely chop eggs.
3. Mix liver, eggs, rice, and oil.
4. Blend in powdered eggshells.

Recipe 90: Feline diabetes dinner No. 1

Cats with diabetes often need more protein and better fiber in their diets to slow the processing of glucose in their systems.

Ingredients:

- 1 pound chicken
- 1 cup chicken livers
- 1 stalk celery
- 1 cup cooked brown rice (not white), cooked in low-sodium chicken broth
- 1 teaspoon eggshell powder
- 1,000 mg taurine

Directions:

1. Boil chicken, chicken livers, and celery together for 20 minutes.
2. Drain, and allow cooling.
3. Chop chicken, chicken livers, and celery into small, kitty-bite-sized pieces.
4. Thoroughly mix all ingredients together with the eggshell powder and taurine.

Recipe 91: Feline diabetes dinner No. 2

Ingredients:

- ½ pound ground chicken (or turkey)
- 1 egg
- 4 ounce canned tuna in oil
- 2 tablespoons cooked broccoli
- 1 teaspoon powdered eggshells
- 1,000 mg taurine

Directions:

1. Scramble egg.
2. Fry chicken; when almost completely done, stir in the egg and cooked broccoli.
3. Continue cooking until chicken is browned, and egg is done.
4. Sprinkle with eggshell powder and taurine.

Recipe 92: Treats for a dairy-tolerant diabetic cat

Ingredients:

- 3+ cups crushed whole oats
- ½ cup Parmesan cheese
- ¼ cup canned pumpkin (not pie filling
- 2 egg yolks
- Water as necessary

Directions

1. Preheat oven to 350° F.
2. Mix all ingredients until they clump together.
3. If more liquid is needed, add in more water.
4. If more dry ingredients are needed, add in more crushed whole oats.
5. Drop by teaspoonfuls onto cookie sheet covered with non-stick spray.
6. Bake for 10 to 12 minutes.

Crock-pot recipes

Use a 4- to 6-quart Crock-pot for the following recipes. Many can be made in the morning, then when you return back to your home in the evening, they are either completely done, or they need just one or two more ingredients added. Your home will smell delicious to your cat, which could be a potential danger. If using a Crock-pot while simultaneously leaving the house, you risk kitty deciding whatever is in that funny-looking bowl on the counter smells too good to be true. Your cat may be tempted to pry open the lid. Because of that potential of getting hurt, if you leave your cat alone while the food cooks, you may want to keep him or her confined to an area away from it. A special note on Crock-pots — because the food cooks for such a long time on relatively low heat settings, they are perfect for preparing vegetables for your cat. They will have a very soft, easily chewable consistency and be more easily digested.

Recipe 93: Beef and rice

Ingredients:

- 1 ½ pounds beef, any kind cut in chunks
- 1 tablespoon chicken fat or fish oil
- 2 carrots, cubed
- 2 yellow summer squash, cubed
- 6 cups broth
- ½ cup cooked rice
- 1 teaspoon eggshell powder
- 1,000 mg taurine

Directions:

1. Brown the meat in a skillet, ensuring all sides are seared.
2. Place the meat in the Crock-pot first, top with the oil, and layer the carrots and squash on top.
3. Pour in all the broth.
4. Cover, and cook on low-heat setting for 8 to 10 hours, or on high-heat setting for 4 to 5 hours.

5. Add in the rice and turn off the unit.

6. When food has cooled enough to pour into your food processor, process by pulsing until it is in chunks small enough for your cat's liking.

7. Add in the eggshell powder and taurine.

Recipe 94: Venison stew

Ingredients:

- 2 pounds venison stew meat
- 2 tablespoons chicken fat
- 3 stalks celery
- 1 tablespoon chopped fresh parsley
- 1 cup beef broth
- 1 teaspoon eggshell powder
- 1,000 mg taurine

Directions:

1. Melt the oil in a skillet on a stove, and brown the venison.

2. Place celery and parsley in Crock-pot, put the browned venison on top.

3. Cover with water.

4. Cook over low heat for 7 to 10 hours.

5. Remove, and pulverize in a processor.

Recipe 95: Bison with vegetables and rice

Ingredients:

- 3 to 4 pounds bison roast, cubed
- 2 tablespoons melted chicken fat
- 2 carrots, cubed
- 2 stalks celery, cubed
- 6 cups beef broth
- ½ cup cooked rice
- 1 tablespoon eggshell powder
- 1,000 mg taurine

Directions:

1. Brown the meat in the fat in a skillet, ensuring all sides are seared.
2. Put vegetables in the Crock-pot, and cover with the meat.
3. Pour in the broth, ensuring everything is covered.
4. Cook on low heat for 8 to 10 hours.
5. Remove from Crock-pot, and mince everything together, or pulverize in a processor.

Recipe 96: Beef, potatoes, and vegetables

Throwing in a bone to this soup gives it more of a meaty flavor. If your cat is a beef lover, he or she will be pleased with your efforts on this.

Ingredients:

- 2 to 2 ½ pounds beef, any kind, cut into chunks
- 1 shank bone (ask your butcher to set one aside for you)
- 1 tablespoon chicken fat or fish oil
- 2 carrots, cubed
- 2 celery stalks, cut up in chunks
- 2 large potatoes
- 6 cups broth
- 1 teaspoon eggshell powder
- 1,000 mg taurine

Directions:

1. Brown the meat in a skillet, ensuring all sides are seared.
2. Place the meat in the Crock-pot first, then the oil, and layer the carrots and squash on top.
3. Pour in all the broth. If more liquid is needed to cover ingredients, add enough water.
4. Cover and cook on low-heat setting for 8 to 10 hours, or on high-heat setting for 4 to 5 hours.
5. Remove, and discard the bone.
6. When food has cooled enough to pour into your food processor, process by pulsing until it is in chunks small enough for your cat's liking.
7. Add in the eggshell powder and taurine.

Recipe 97: Lamb and oats with vegetables

Ingredients:

- 1 ½ pounds lamb stew meat cut into 1-inch chunks
- ½ cup whole oats
- 1 tablespoon chicken fat or fish oil
- 2 carrots, cubed
- 2 celery stalks, cut up in chunks
- 4 cups beef broth
- 1 teaspoon eggshell powder
- 1,000 mg taurine

Directions:

1. Place the meat, oats, fat or oil, and vegetables in the Crock-pot.
2. Pour in the broth.
3. Cover, and cook on low-heat setting for 6 to 8 hours, or on high-heat setting for 3 to 4 hours.
4. When food has cooled enough to pour into your food processor, process by pulsing until it is in hunks small enough for your cat's liking.
5. Add in the eggshell powder and taurine.

Recipe 98: Stewed chicken

Ingredients:

- 4 to 4 ½ pounds whole chicken, including the innards
- 2 carrots, cubed
- 2 celery stalks, cut up in chunks
- 4 cups water or onion-free, salt-free vegetable broth
- 1 teaspoon eggshell powder
- 1,000 mg taurine

Directions:

1. Cut the chicken into quarters.
2. Place chicken with vegetables into Crock-pot, cover with water.
3. Cover, and cook for 7 to 10 hours on high heat, or 3 ½ to 5 hours on low.
4. Remove chicken.
5. When chicken is cool enough to touch, remove the meat from the bone.
6. Discard all bones.
7. Pulverize chicken in a food processor.
8. Add in carrots, celery, and broth, and pulse until all are mixed and mashed thoroughly.
9. Add in the eggshell powder and taurine.

Recipe 99: Turkey and rice

Ingredients:

- 1 pound turkey thighs or breasts, or a combination, cut in large chunks
- 2 carrots, cubed
- 2 celery stalks, cut up in chunks
- 1 cup uncooked rice
- 4 cups chicken or turkey broth
- 1 teaspoon eggshell powder
- 1,000 mg taurine

Directions:

1. Place turkey, vegetables, and rice into Crock-pot.
2. Cover with broth, adding water if necessary.
3. Cover, and cook on low for 7 to 8 hours, or on high for 3 ½ to 4 hours.
4. Remove, and process in a food processor until food is a consistency your cat prefers.
5. Stir in the eggshell powder and taurine.

Other Natural Remedies

Recipe 100: Odor remover

This recipe should be made only when it is needed. The hydrogen peroxide will lose its effectiveness after being exposed to the air for 30 minutes.

Warning: You cannot seal the container you mix it in. The baking soda contains sodium bicarbonate. It will create an expanding chemical compound when combined with the hydrogen peroxide. If placed in a container with a lid, you risk a small, but dangerous, explosion. Stir ingredients in a glass bowl with a wooden spoon.

Ingredients:

- ½ cup hydrogen peroxide (3 percent)
- ½ teaspoon baking soda
- 1 drop dishwashing liquid

Directions:

1. Stir all ingredients in a glass container with a wooden spoon (as it is non-reactive).

2. Apply the solution with a cloth to the plastic of the litter box, and allow to air dry.

Note: This can also be used to clean carpets or upholstered areas that have been "sprayed" by your cat. Sop up the excess, without completely blotting, with a clean cloth, and reapply as necessary. Be sure to do a colorfast test in an inconspicuous area prior to using it in the middle of your living room.

Recipe 101: All-purpose cleaner

Though this recipe is not for when you need to disinfect your kitchen counters, it will not kill bacteria, so it would not be good to use after you have cut up chicken on the counter. But for daily maintenance, it is ideal and will not put toxins on kitty's feet when he or she walks across them to do the daily kitchen inspection. It is good for counters, tile, or linoleum floors, and other non-porous surfaces.

Ingredients:

- 1 cup white vinegar
- ½ cup baking soda
- 1 gallon water

Directions:

1. Simple: stir all ingredients together.
2. You can pour this into a spray bottle and keep indefinitely.

APPENDIX

Sample
Food Diary Page

Date	Event	Reaction
7/18/10	Made and froze Chicken-rice meal	
	Fed beaf and lamb	Did not like it. Ate just a little.
7/19/10	breakfast: turkey & pumpkin	loved it, no trouble
	dinner: turkey - tuna surprise	again loved it, must really like turkey
7/20/10	Vet appointment	Lost 1/2 pound since last check up!
	Breakfast: Scrambled eggs with liver added	Lapped it up, but gas later

Shopping List

Protein sources:

- ❏ Chicken
- ❏ Cornish game hen
- ❏ Beef
- ❏ Bison
- ❏ Venison
- ❏ Emu
- ❏ Goat
- ❏ Guinea fowl
- ❏ Lamb
- ❏ Mice and other rodents (e.g., gopher, vole)
- ❏ Quail, pheasant, and other small birds
- ❏ Rabbit
- ❏ Turkey
- ❏ Eggs
- ❏ Fish
  Wild salmon
  Mackerel
  Canned salmon, mackerel, and tuna

Carbohydrates:

- ❏ Carrots

- ❏ Celery

Cruciferous vegetables (in very small amounts):

- ❏ Broccoli
- ❏ Brussels sprouts
- ❏ Cabbage
- ❏ Kohlrabi
- ❏ Turnips
- ❏ Green beans

Grasses and greens:

- ❏ Collard greens
- ❏ Dandelion greens
- ❏ Kale
- ❏ Swiss chard
- ❏ Rye grass
- ❏ Barley grass
- ❏ Wheatgrass
- ❏ Catnip
- ❏ Peas
- ❏ Pumpkin
- ❏ Summer squash
- ❏ Zucchini

- ❏ Sweet potatoes
- ❏ Winter squash
- ❏ Basil
- ❏ Oregano
- ❏ Parsley
- ❏ Acorn squash
- ❏ Butternut squash
- ❏ White potatoes
- ❏ Rice
- ❏ Rice bran
- ❏ Ground eggshells
- ❏ Cottage cheese
- ❏ Heavy cream
- ❏ Whole Italian cheeses (Parmesan, asiago, pecorino, Romano)
- ❏ Brewer's yeast or nutritional yeast
- ❏ Bonito fish flakes
- ❏ Pumpkin seeds
- ❏ Sesame seeds
- ❏ Rice flour

BIBLIOGRAPHY

Lappin, Michael. *Feline Internal Medicine Secrets: Questions you will be asked on rounds, in the clinic and on exams.* Philadelphia: Hanley & Belfus, Inc. 2001

Nutrient Requirements of Dogs and Cats. National Academies Press, 500 Fifth Street, NW, Washington, DC 20001. **www.nap.edu**

Robinson, D. S., and Eskin, N. A. *Oxidative Enzymes in Foods.* London: Escvier, 1991, p. 49.

RESOURCES

Veterinary Botanical Medical Association: **www.vbma.org**

National Animal Supplement Council: **www.nasc.cc**

The National Academies: **www.national-academiew.org**

North American Society of Homeopaths: **www.homeopathy.org**

Online sources of raw meats:

> Meat for Cats and Dogs: **www.meatforcatsanddogs.com**
>
> Only Natural Pet Store: **www.onlynaturalpet.com**
>
> Dog Gone Natural: **www.doggonenatural.com**
>
> VIP Pet Supplies: **www.vippetsupplies.com**

Online sources for meat grinders:

> Everything Kitchens: **www.everythingkitchens.com**
>
> LEM™ Products: **www.lemproducts.com**
>
> Northern Tool Products: **www.northerntool.com**
>
> Food Shopping Network: **www.foodnetworkstore.com**

Online sources for tabletop water fountains:

> Serenity Health: **www.serenityhealth.com**

Kinetic Fountains: **www.kineticfountains.com**

Relaxing Water Fountains: **www.relaxingwaterfountains.com**

Aqua Arts for Home: **www.aquaarts.com**

Online sources for Yunnan Paiyao:

Suigetsu Shop: **www.shopsuigetsu.com**

Shenyi Center of Chinese Medicine:
www.helpofchinesemedicine.com

Very Asia: **www.veryasia.com**

AUTHOR BIOGRAPHY

Lisa Shiroff is a writer and animal lover living in the suburbs of Philadelphia with her husband, two kids, and a couple of questionably alive hermit crabs. Yes, she's currently catless, but that's just a matter of timing.

INDEX

Singapura 24
slippery elm bark 121, 263
sodium 46, 266, 275
Sojourner Farms 85
Spratt, James 66
squamous cell carcinoma 152
stevia 118, 160
struvite 54, 145

T

taurine 19, 32, 33, 34, 51, 52, 54, 55,
57, 77, 96, 136, 149, 151, 155,
156, 177, 199, 214, 215, 216,
217, 218, 220, 221, 222, 223,
224, 225, 226, 227, 228, 229,
230, 231, 232, 233, 234, 235,
236, 237, 238, 249, 250, 251,
252, 253, 254, 255, 256, 257,
258, 259, 260, 261, 262, 263,
264, 266, 267, 268, 269, 270,
271, 272, 273, 274, 288
theobromine 56
thiamine 49, 59
turmeric 137

U

undercoat hair 26
U.S. Wellness Meats 77

V

Veterinary
Botanical Medicine Association
120
Emergency and Critical Care
Society (VECCS) 63
vitamin
A 48, 53, 57, 87

B1 59
vitamin B6 50
B12 50
D 48, 49, 53
E 47, 49, 111
K 49

W

weaning 102, 106, 109
Wild Kitty 83, 84

Z

zinc 47, 62